DIY PROJECTS
for the
Self-Sufficient
Homeowner

25 WAYS TO BUILD A
SELF-RELIANT LIFESTYLE

COOL
SPRINGS
PRESS
Growing Successful Gardeners™

MINNEAPOLIS, MINNESOTA

First Published in 2011 by Cool Springs Press,
an imprint of Quarto Publishing Group USA Inc.,
400 First Avenue North, Suite 400,
Minneapolis, MN 55401 USA.

Printed in China

20 19

Library of Congress Cataloging-in-Publication Data

Matheson, Betsy.
 DIY projects for the self-sufficient homeowner : 25 ways to
build a self-reliant lifestyle / by Betsy Matheson.
    p. cm.
 Summary: "Step-by-step, how-to projects for home rain
collection, solar panels, food storage, solar energy systems,
eco-friendly improvements, bee keeping, and more"--
Provided by publisher.
 Includes index.
 ISBN-13: 978-1-58923-567-0 (soft cover)
 ISBN-10: 1-58923-567-3 (soft cover)
 1. Ecological houses--Design and construction. 2. Sustainable
living. I. Title.

TH4860.M386 2011
643'.7--dc22
                              2010042928

President/CEO: Ken Fund

Home Improvement Group

Publisher: Bryan Trandem
Managing Editor: Tracy Stanley
Senior Editor: Mark Johanson
Creative Director: Michele Lanci-Altomare
Art Direction/Design: Brad Springer, Jon Simpson, James Kegley
Lead Photographer: Joel Schnell
Set Builder: James Parmeter
Production Managers: Laura Hokkanen, Linda Halls

Author: Betsy Matheson Symanietz
Text Design: Lois Stanfield
Page Layout Artist: Lois Stanfield
Tech Editor: Eric Smith
Shop Help: Charles Boldt
Proofreader: Leah Cochenet Noel
Photography: Carolyn Henry-Johanson
Photo Help: Christensen Family—Scott, Lisa, Tait, Sophie;
Jacquie Johnson; Springer Family—Nona, Hannah, Hayley,
Helena; Scott Travis; John P. Keane; Jason Remington;
Dustin Denison; Therese Krupp

Contents

Introduction   5

DIY PROJECTS

1 ○ Collecting Rainwater   13

2 ○ Collecting Gray Water   19

3 ○ Composting   23

4 ○ Raised Beds   33

5 ○ Container Gardening   39

6 ○ Building a Cold Frame   49

7 ○ Starting & Transplanting Seedlings   55

8 ○ Building a Greenhouse   59

9 ○ Building a Hoophouse   69

10 ○ Preserving Your Bounty   79

11 ○ Setting Up a Root Cellar   93

12 ○ Raising Animals   103

13 ○ Building a Chicken Ark   115

14 ○ Building a Beehive   126

15 ○ Solar Electricity   131

16 ○ Solar Security Light Circuit   141

17 ○ Solar Heat   149

Index   159

Declare Your Independence

The world seems to be growing in complexity every day. While much of today's new technology makes legitimate improvements in our lives, this new electronic age has created something of a backlash. Each upgraded cellphone generation and ever-spreading factory farm distances us just a little bit farther from the days when all you needed to conquer the world was a tillable acre and a mule. The projects in this book are designed to help you close that widening gap—if only just a bit.

The decisions we make every day—even down to which grain was used to make the flour in your morning toast—are part of a chain of thousands of other decisions that, taken together, have a profound effect on the resources of our planet and the health and prosperity of our families. The urge to take back some control of our own lives and futures has never been stronger.

The good news is: You can. Whether you live in a bustling city, sprawling suburban development, or rural estate, you can achieve greater everyday self-sufficiency with relatively little effort. As self-sufficiency expert John Seymour wrote, "You do not need five acres and a degree in horticulture to become self-sufficient … self-sufficiency is about taking control and becoming an effective producer of whatever your resources allow."

DIY Projects for the Self-Sufficient Homeowner provides you with around two dozen ways to help you maximize your resources and participate in the march toward greater

TIP

Self-Sufficiency vs. Green

People who are interested in adopting a more self-sufficient lifestyle almost certainly subscribe to today's Green principles and to an approach to living based on stewardship. It is worth noting, however, that the projects described in this book were chosen because they result in a product, usually a consumable, that contributes directly to the pool of things you and your family need in order to live—and live well.

Solar panels that collect and heat air to warm cold spaces in your home are mechanisms you can build yourself and duct in to your home's existing ductwork. Learn how on page 147.

self-reliance. Whether you own a small balcony downtown or a couple of acres in the suburbs, you can grow much more of your own food than you ever expected—as long as you have the right tools, such as raised garden beds, compost bins, container gardens, or even a small greenhouse. Whether you have an expansive estate or a small backyard, you can raise animals—this book will show you how to build a chicken coop, a beehive, and animal-friendly fencing. It contains many more projects related to the production and storage of food from your own homestead.

But raising your own food is not the only way to increase your self-reliance. With new DIY-friendly technology, generating your own clean energy is easier than ever. Here, you'll see exactly how to build a solar panel, install solar energy systems, and understand alternative energy sources.

The key to your self-sufficiency is to focus first on a few doable projects that fit into your lifestyle without a lot of adjustments. Most modern homeowners will not be able to maintain a fully self-sufficient home without quitting their day job, and that shouldn't necessarily be the goal for everyone. All homeowners can, however, take steps toward greater self-reliance, and partake in the satisfaction that comes from providing for your family's needs through your own effort. So get started: The time has never been better to declare your independence.

○ The Self-Sufficient Lifestyle

Self-sufficient living is a highly complementary practice—once you begin, you'll find that many parts of your home are connected, and that multiple systems of self-sufficiency contribute to one another, often corresponding with the natural cycles of the earth.

Because of this interconnectedness, many of the projects in this book will naturally lead you to more and more projects that will help you maximize your self-sufficiency work.

For example, if you start a garden, the fruits and vegetables you grow will provide waste that will transform into the compost that will nurture next year's bounty. Setting up a rainwater collection system not only reduces your reliance on public utilities, the fresh, soft water will help your plants grow healthy. The hens you are raising for their eggs control garden pests and provide free fertilizer. At the end of the growing season, you'll likely be overwhelmed with vegetables, and will need to find a means to store and preserve them—perhaps a basement root cellar could be a good option. And, by growing organic vegetables nurtured by compost and animal manure, you create a pesticide-free habitat for honeybees to prosper, while they, in turn, pollinate the plant life.

That said, you do not need to take on all the projects in this book at once. Start with the projects that naturally supplement the efforts your family is already making toward self-sufficiency. If you already recycle, a natural next step is to build compost bins and begin to make compost with food and paper waste as well. If you already maintain a beautiful flower garden, why not build a home for the honeybees that are already

Building a greenhouse is a great way for gardeners to jump-start the growing season, or to introduce new, sensitive plants to your garden. See page 59.

frequent visitors, allowing you to collect the honey they produce? If you need to connect electricity to an outbuilding or shed that is not currently grid-connected, why not install solar panels instead of wiring the building into the grid? If you already garden, why not build a greenhouse?

For the newcomer, the projects on the following pages provide multiple opportunities to create a more self-reliant lifestyle. For the experienced self-sufficient homeowner, the step-by-step projects included here will provide you with the means to expand and streamline your efforts.

○ Efficiency, Conservation & Recycling

If increased self-sufficiency is your goal, paying attention to the efficiency with which you use your resources is common sense. For example, if your goal is to use solar-heated air to heat all or part of your home, it makes sense that you want every bit of the heat your solar panels produce to contribute to the temperature of the room, instead of being lost through drafty windows or poorly insulated walls. Investing in energy-efficient windows and doors and properly insulating your home is a very important step in the implementation of an alternate or supplementary heating system.

If one of the goals of your self-sufficient lifestyle is to decrease your utility bills, a key first step that is often overlooked is resource conservation, which can make a huge and immediate impact on your utility bills. For example, before you invest in a gray water recycling system or install a cistern for rainwater collection to lessen your dependence on water provided by utility companies, coach your family in water conservation practices. Run the dishwasher only when it is full, wash only full loads of laundry, turn off the tap when brushing your teeth, and focus on taking shorter, more efficient showers.

Increasing your own awareness of how to reuse the objects around you to benefit your self-sufficient living projects will also contribute to your success as a self-sufficient homeowner. If you plan to start your own seedlings each year, you'll need planting containers. Why not reuse plastic yogurt cups or other food containers you've already used instead of purchasing new containers? One of the nuggets of wisdom modern self-reliant homeowners must adopt is that objects do not need to be as disposable as we are led to believe. Find a way to repurpose the objects you buy, compost paper and food waste, and ensure that your tools, buildings and appliances are properly maintained to ensure that they enjoy a long and useful life in your home.

The best resources are the ones you already own. Re-using or repurposing stuff you no longer need takes some creativity, but ultimately it fills needs, not landfills. For example, this discarded dressing table found new life as a vanity cabinet in a self-sufficient homeowner's bathroom.

○ Getting Started

A key factor in finding your starting point is to develop an understanding of your goals as a self-sufficient homeowner. Self-sufficiency can contribute to many different aspects of your family's lifestyle. So before you plot out your projects, consider the tenets of self-sufficiency, as described below, and define what being self-sufficient means to you.

Producing Your Own Food: This is unquestionably the most involved aspect of a self-sufficient lifestyle for many homeowners—urban, suburban, and rural. Consider how food production and storage can fit into your home, whether you plan to start a garden or build a greenhouse, raise chickens and other small animals, build a root cellar for winter produce storage, or raise honeybees.

Saving on Utility Costs: Independence from local energy sources is another major draw for self-reliance enthusiasts. Whether you seek independence from utility companies because of prohibitive costs, unreliable service, or your own desire to live off the grid, many of the projects in this book can help you take first steps to get there. Bear in mind, however, that many energy- or utility-production systems do require a significant financial investment in the beginning, but will pay for themselves within the first ten years of use.

Producing Clean Energy: Many self-sufficient homeowners are more motivated by their desire to produce energy for their homes with little or no impact on the environment than they are by utility company bills. Producing non-polluting, renewable energy is increasingly achievable for residential homeowners as technological advances make the necessary equipment affordable, accessible, and easy to install.

Conserving Resources and Creating Less Waste: Conserving the earth's resources and minimizing waste is a practice that goes hand-in-hand with a self-sufficient lifestyle.

Building your own chicken coop is a great project for DIYers of all skill levels (see page 115). Chickens provide nutritious eggs, natural garden pest-control, and organic fertilizer.

Collected rainwater is perfect for watering the garden or the lawn. Rain is soft and free of most pollutants, so it is perfect for plant irrigation. Learn how to make your own rain barrels—flip to page 13.

Drying produce is one way to preserve the fruits of your labor, so you can enjoy your garden's bounty through the winter months. Learn how to build a simple solar food dryer on page 86.

Even if you don't have a lot of space, you can use any sunny spot to grow produce in containers. A strawberry barrel like this can house up to 25 feet of strawberry plants and only takes up 2 square feet of space. To make your own barrel, see page 46.

DIY Projects

Collecting Rainwater

Practically everything around your house that requires water loves the natural goodness that's provided with soft rainwater. With a simple rain barrel, you can collect rainwater to irrigate your garden or lawn, water your houseplants, or top off swimming pools and hot tubs. A ready supply of rainwater is also a reliable stand-by for emergency use if your primary water supply is interrupted.

Collecting rainwater runoff in rain barrels can save thousands of gallons of tap water each year. A typical 40 × 40-ft. roof is capable of collecting 1,000 gallons of water from only one inch of rain. A large rainwater collection system that squeezes every drop from your roof can provide most—or sometimes all—of the water used throughout the home, if it's combined with large cisterns, pumps, and purification processing.

Sprinkling your lawn and garden can consume as much as 40 percent of the total household water use during the growing season. A simple rain barrel system that limits collected water to outdoor (nonpotable) use only, like the rain barrels described on the following pages, can have a big impact on the self-sufficiency of your home, helping you save on utility expenses and reducing the energy used to process and purify water for your lawn and garden. Some communities now offer subsidies for rain barrel use, offering free or reduced-price barrels and downspout connection kits. Check with your local water authority for more information. Get smart with your water usage, and take advantage of the abundant supply from above.

Rainwater that is collected in a rain barrel before it hits the ground is free of many contaminants that water picks up as it filters through soil. This soft, warm (and free) water is perfect for plants, lawns, and many other outdoor applications.

○ Rain Barrels

Rain barrels, either built from scratch or purchased as a kit, are a great way to irrigate a lawn or garden without running up your utilities bill. The most common systems include one or more rain barrels (40 to 80 gallons) positioned below gutter downspouts to collect water runoff from the roof. A hose or drip irrigation line can be connected to spigot valves at the bottom of the rain barrel. You can use a single barrel, or connect several rain barrels in series to collect and dispense even more rainwater.

Plastic rain barrel kits are available for purchase at many home centers for around $100. If kit prices aren't for you, a rain barrel is easy to make yourself for a fraction of the price. The most important component to your homemade barrel is the drum you choose.

Obtaining a Barrel

Practically any large waterproof container can be used to make a rain barrel. One easily obtained candidate is a trash can, preferably plastic, with a snap-on lid. A standard 32-gallon can will work for a rain barrel, but if you can find a 44-gallon can choose it instead. Although wood barrels are becoming more scarce, you can still get them from wineries. A used 55-gallon barrel can be obtained free or for a small charge from a bulk food supplier. Most 55-gallon barrels today are plastic, but some metal barrels are still floating around. Whatever the material, make sure the barrel did not contain any chemical or compound that could be harmful to plants, animals, or humans. If you don't know what was in it, don't use it. Choose a barrel made out of opaque material that lets as little light through as possible, reducing the risk of algae growth.

A barrelful of water is an appealing breeding ground for mosquitoes and a perfect incubator for algae. Filters and screens over the barrel opening should prevent insect infestation, but for added protection against mosquitoes add one tablespoon of vegetable oil to the water in the barrel. This coats the top surface of the stored water and deprives the larvae of oxygen.

TOOLS & MATERIALS

Barrel or trash can

Drill with spade bit

Jigsaw

Hole saw

Barb fitting with nut for overflow hose

1½" sump drain hose for overflow

¾" hose bibb or sillcock

¾" male pipe coupling

¾" bushing or bulkhead connector

Channel-type pliers

Fiberglass window screening

Cargo strap with ratchet

Teflon tape

Silicone caulk

How to Make a Rain Barrel

1 Cut a large opening in the barrel top or lid. Mark the size and shape of your opening—if using a bulk food barrel, mark a large semi-circle in the top of the barrel. If using a plastic garbage can with a lid, mark a 12"-dia. circle in the center of the lid. Drill a starter hole, and then cut out the shape with a jigsaw.

2 Install the overflow hose. Drill a hole near the top of the barrel for the overflow fitting. Thread the barb fitting into the hole and secure it to the barrel on the inside with the retainer nut and rubber washer (if provided). Slide the overflow hose into the barbed end of the barb elbow until the end of the hose seats against the elbow flange.

Sillcock
Coupling
Connector

3 Drill the access hole for the spigot (either a hose bibb or sillcock, brass or PVC). Tighten the stem of the sillcock onto a threaded coupling inserted into the access hole. Inside the barrel, a rubber washer is slipped onto the coupling end and then a threaded bushing is tightened over the coupling to create a seal. Apply a strip of Teflon tape to all threaded parts before making each connection. Caulk around the spigot with clear silicone caulk.

4 Screen over the opening in the top of the barrel. Lay a piece of fiberglass insect mesh over the top of the trash can and secure it around the rim with a cargo strap or bungee cord that can be drawn drum-tight. Snap the trash can lid over the top. Once you have installed the rain barrel, periodically remove and clean the mesh.

How to Install a Rain Barrel

Whether you purchase a rain barrel or make your own from scratch or a kit, how well it meets your needs will depend on where you put it and how it is set up. Some rain barrels are temporary holding tanks that store water runoff just long enough to direct it into your yard through a hose and drip irrigation head. Other rain barrels are more of a reservoir that supplies water on-demand by filling up watering cans or buckets. If you plan to use the spigot as the primary means for dispensing water, you'll want to position the rain barrel well off the ground for easy access (raising your rain barrel has no effect on water pressure).

In addition to height, other issues surrounding the placement of your rain barrel (or rain barrels) include the need to provide a good base, orientation of the spigot and overflow, the position relative to your downspouts, and how to link more than one rain barrel together. **TIP**: Wherever possible, locate your rain barrel in a shaded area. Sunlight encourages algae growth, especially in barrels that are partially translucent.

TOOLS & MATERIALS

Drill/driver

Screwdriver

Hack saw

Rainbarrel

Hose & fittings

Base material (pavers)

Downspout adapter and extension

Teflon tape

1 Select a location for the barrel under a downspout. Locate your barrel as close to the area you want to irrigate as possible. Make sure the barrel has a stable, level base.

2 Install the spigot. Some kits may include a second spigot for filling watering cans. Use Teflon tape at all threaded fittings to ensure a tight seal. Connect the overflow tube, and make sure it is pointed away from the foundation.

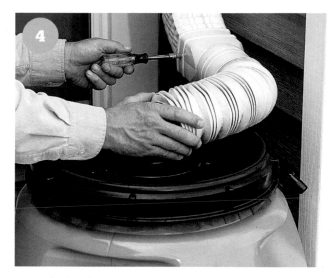

3 Cut the downspout to length with a hacksaw. Reconnect the elbow fitting to the downspout using sheet-metal screws. Attach the cover to the top of the rain barrel. Some systems include a cover with porous wire mesh, to which the downspout delivers water. Others include a cover with a sealed connection (next step).

4 Link the downspout elbow to the rain barrel with a length of flexible downspout extension attached to the elbow and the barrel cover.

Variation: If your barrel comes with a downspout adapter, cut away a segment of downspout and insert the adapter so it diverts water into the barrel.

5 Connect a drip irrigation tube or garden hose to the spigot. A Y-fitting, like the one shown here, will let you feed the drip irrigation system through a garden hose when the rain barrel is empty.

6 If you want, increase water storage by connecting two or more rain barrels together with a linking kit, available from many kit suppliers.

To reservoir with
overflow protection

Collecting Gray Water

Gray water is a term used to describe wastewater from your water source that is free of contaminants like toilet waste and garbage disposal remains. Water that has come into contact with these types of contaminants is referred to as "black water" and its reuse is strictly prohibited for public health reasons. Wastewater generated directly from the tap (usually while you're waiting for the tap water to heat up or cool down) contains very few or no contaminants, such as soap, cleaning chemicals, food waste, or other added organic and inorganic material.

Gray water can be collected easily and used for many household purposes without treatment or filtration. It is not suitable for consumption, however. Gray water that contains some contaminants, such as laundry suds, dish soap, or shower/bath water can be used for some limited purposes, such as flushing toilets.

A simple way to capture gray water for reuse is to install a diverter in the form of a small sink basin and drain. Instead of leading to the sewer, the diverter's drain is directed to a closed receptacle, usually in the basement or outdoors. The captured water can be used for watering plants or the lawn. To avoid allowing bacteria to fester in the gray water receptacle, do not allow the water to stagnate.

A small gray water recovery sink that drains automatically to a reservoir makes it easy to reuse gray water for watering plants or gardens. Gray water systems like this make it easy to recycle thousands of gallons of clean tap water each year.

TIP

Removing a Sprayer

Remove your old sink sprayer to clear an opening for the diverter sink in your sink deck. The hose that supplies the sprayer usually is attached to the base of the faucet valve. You'll need to disconnect it and tighten a screw-on tube cap onto the bottom of the tube.

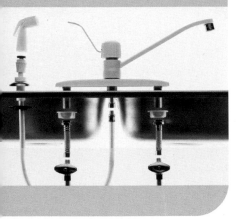

The gray water collection sink seen in this project is a fairly simple technology. Advanced recovery systems are designed to help you reuse wastewater of many types. They are complex and can involve double-plumbing throughout parts of your home, along with water purification processes and chemicals, holding tanks, plumbing switches, pumps, subsurface irrigation systems, and other components. If you're committed to reusing as much water as you can for as many purposes as possible, hire a professional to design the best system for your family's needs.

Installing a Gray Water Recovery Sink

The Envirosink gray water diverter apparatus installed in this project is available for sale online and from "Green" home retailers (See Resources, page 158.) It is designed to be mounted in a kitchen sink deck knockout—usually the one reserved for the sprayer or the soap dispenser. It can be used with any kitchen faucet—you simply spin the faucet to empty into the diverter.

Once it is diverted from the sink drain by the collection sink, the gray water is directed through a hose to a reservoir from which it can be dispensed easily for general household use. The reservoir should be a sealed tank with an overflow fitting that leads to the home drain/waste system (if indoors) or a well-drained runoff area (if outdoors). The plumbing for the runoff system should include a P-trap and an air admittance valve (or other backflow preventer).

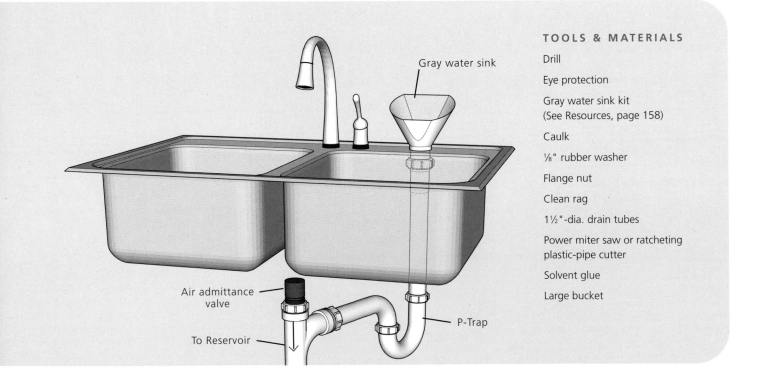

Gray water sink

Air admittance valve

To Reservoir

P-Trap

TOOLS & MATERIALS

Drill

Eye protection

Gray water sink kit (See Resources, page 158)

Caulk

1/8" rubber washer

Flange nut

Clean rag

1½"-dia. drain tubes

Power miter saw or ratcheting plastic-pipe cutter

Solvent glue

Large bucket

How to Install a Gray Water Diverter Sink

1 Choose the best spot for the diverter sink to be mounted. Usually, this means taking over an unused knockout in your sink deck or removing a sprayer or soap dispenser. Otherwise, you can drill a hole for the diverter as close as possible to the diverter.

2 Attach the diverter sink's drain tailpiece to the sink deck or countertop. Apply a small bead of kitchen and bath caulk around the edges of the hole and press the tailpiece flange into the caulk. From below, slip a ⅛" rubber washer onto the tailpiece and then hand-tighten a flange nut.

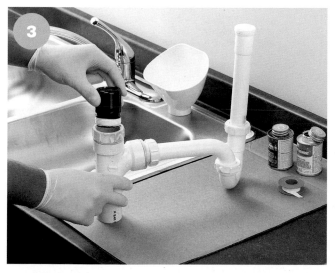

3 Assemble the sink drain system completely before installing it as a unit. Here, an air admittance valve is being solvent-glued to a drain stub from the drain P-trap. You'll need to run additional drain pipe to supply water to your reservoir. Contact a plumbing professional if you do not have experience with home plumbing.

4 Hook up the drain assembly to the tailpiece from the diverter sink. Run drain pipe to your water storage reservoir tank, making sure the tank is equipped with an overflow valve and tubing that leads into the main drain system.

Composting

The byproducts of yard maintenance and food preparation accumulate rapidly. Everyday yardcare alone creates great heaps of grass clippings, trimmings, leaves, branches, and weeds. Add to this the potato peelings, coffee grounds, apple cores, and a host of organic kitchen leavings. The result is a large mass of organic matter that is far too valuable a resource to be simply dumped into the solid waste stream via curbside garbage collection. Yard waste and kitchen scraps can be recycled into compost and incorporated back into planters or garden beds as a nutrient-rich (and cost-free) soil amendment.

Compost is nature's own potting soil, and it effectively increases soil porosity, improves fertility, and stimulates healthy root development. Besides, making your own soil amendment through composting is much less expensive than buying commercial materials.

So how does garbage turn into plant food? The process works like this: Organisms such as bacteria, fungi, worms, and insects convert compost materials into humus, a loamy, nutrient-rich soil. Humus is the end goal of composting. Its production can take a couple of years if left undisturbed, or it can be sped up with some help from your pitchfork and a little livestock manure.

Although composting occurs throughout nature anywhere some organic matter hits the earth, in our yards and gardens it is always a good idea to contain the activity in a designated area, like a compost bin. Functionally, there are two basic kinds of bins: multi-compartment compost factories that require a fair amount of attention from you and hidden heaps where organic matter is discarded to rot at its own pace.

Composting turns yard waste and kitchen scraps into a valuable soil amendment.

Both approaches are valid and both will produce usable compost. The main compost bin project seen on p. 28 is an example of the more passive style. At roughly one cubic yard in volume, it can handle most of your household organic waste and some garden waste. If you have a higher volume of organic waste or want to use a three-bin approach to staged composting, simply build additional bins.

○ Compost Variables

Air: The best microbes for decomposing plant materials are aerobic, meaning they need oxygen. Without air, aerobic microbes die and their anaerobic cousins take over. Anaerobic microbes thrive without oxygen and decompose materials by putrefaction, which is smelly and slow. Your goal is aerobic activity, which smells musty and loamy, like wet leaves. Improve air circulation in your compost bin by ensuring air passageways are never blocked. Intersperse layers of heavier ingredients (grass clippings, wet leaves) with lighter materials like straw, and turn the pile periodically with a garden fork or pitchfork to promote air circulation.

Water: Compost should be as wet as a wrung-out sponge. A pile that's too wet chokes out necessary air. A too-dry pile will compost too slowly. When adding water to a compost pile, wet in layers, first spraying the pile with a hose, then adding a layer of materials.

Temperature: A fast-composting pile produces quite a bit of heat. On a cool morning, you might notice steam rising from the pile. This is a good sign. Track the temperature of your pile and you'll know how well it's progressing. Aim for a constant temperature between 140 and 150 degrees Fahrenheit, not to exceed 160 degrees. To warm up a cool pile, agitate it to increase air circulation and add nitrogen-dense materials like kitchen waste or grass clippings. A pile about three feet high and wide will insulate the middle of the pile and prevent heat from escaping. You'll know the compost process is complete when the pile looks like dirt and is no longer generating extraordinary heat.

Called "black gold" by home gardeners, compost can be generated on-site and added to any planting bed, lawn, or container for a multitude of benefits. Sifting the compost before you introduce it to your yard or garden is recommended.

○ Browns and Greens

A fast-burning compost pile requires a healthy balance of "browns" and "greens." Browns are high in carbon, which food energy microorganisms depend on to decompose the pile. Greens are high in nitrogen, which is a protein source for the multiplying microbes. A ratio of three-to-one brown-to-green materials is a good target.

Browns: Dry brown plant material, straw, dried brown weeds, wood chips, some saw dust (use with caution—avoid saw dust from chemically treated wood)

Greens: Grass clippings, kitchen fruit and vegetable scraps, green leaves, and manure

Note: If you use chemical lawn care products on your lawn, do not include grass clippings in your compost pile.

Building a Compost Bin

CUTTING LIST

Key	Part	No.	Dim.	Material
A	Post	8	1½ × 1¾ × 48"	Cedar
B	Door rail	2	1½ × 3½ × 16"	"
C	Door rail	2	1½ × 1¾ × 16"	"
D	Door stile	4	1½ × 1¾ × 30½"	"
E	Panel rail	3	1½ × 3½ × 32½"	"
F	Panel rail	3	1½ × 1¾ × 32½"	"
G	Panel stile	3	1½ × 3½ × 30½"	"
H	Infill	16	¾ × 1½ × 30½"	"
I	Filler	80	¾ × 1½ × 4"	"
J	Panel grid	12	¾ × 1½" × Cut to fit	"

Key	Part	No.	Dim.	Material
K	Grid frame-v	16	¾ × 1½" × Cut to fit	Cedar
L	Door frame-h	4	¾ × 1½" × Cut to fit	"
M	Top rail-side	2	1½ × 1¾ × 39"	"
N	Top rail-back	1	1½ × 1¾ × 32½"	"
O	Front spreader	1	1½ × 3½ × 32½"	"

Also need:
½" galvanized hardware cloth 36" by 12 ft.
U-nails (fence staples)
2 pairs 2 × 2" butt hinges
2½" deck screws
Exterior wood glue
Galvanized finish screws
Exterior wood sealant

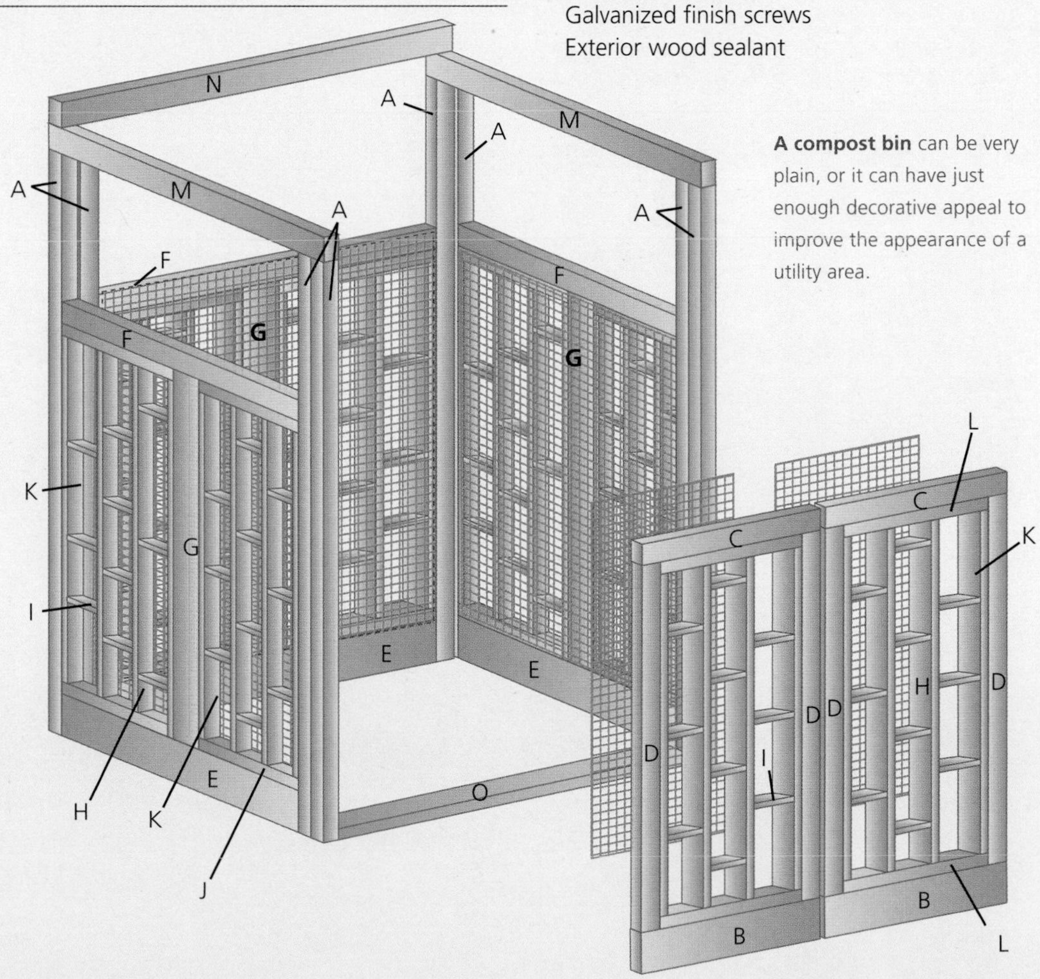

A compost bin can be very plain, or it can have just enough decorative appeal to improve the appearance of a utility area.

How to Build a Compost Bin

1 Prepare the wood stock. At most building centers and lumber yards, you can buy cedar sanded on all four sides, or with one face left rough. The dimensions in this project are sanded on all four sides. Prepare the wood by ripping some of the stock into 1¾"-wide strips (do this by ripping 2 × 4s down the middle on a tablesaw or with a circular saw and cutting guide).

2 Cut the parts to length with a power miter saw or a circular saw. For uniform results, set up a stop block and cut all similar parts at once.

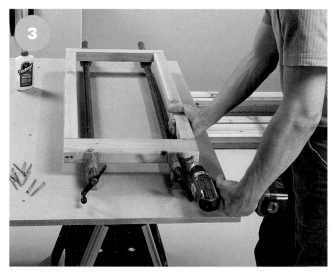

3 Assemble the door frames. Apply exterior-rated wood glue to the mating parts and clamp them together with pipe or bar clamps. Reinforce the top joints with 3" countersunk deck screws (two per joint). Reinforce the bottom joints by drilling a pair of ⅜"-dia. × 1" deep clearance holes up through the bottom edges of the bottom rails and then driving 3" deck screws through these holes up into the stiles.

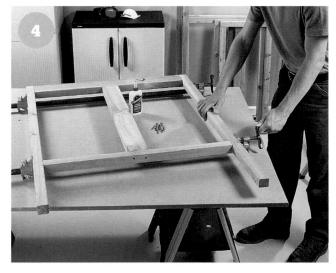

4 Assemble the side and back panels. Clamp and glue the posts and rails for each frame, making sure the joints are square. Then, reinforce the joints with countersunk 3" deck screws.

5 Hang the door frames. With the posts cut to length and oriented correctly, attach a door frame to each post with a pair of galvanized butt hinges. The bottoms of the door frames should be slightly higher than the bottoms of the posts. Temporarily tack a 1 × 4 brace across both door bottom rails to keep the doors from swinging during construction.

6 Join the panels and the door assembly by gluing and clamping the parts together and then driving 2½" countersunk deck screws to reinforce the joints. To stabilize the assembly, fasten the 2 × 4 front spreader between the front, bottom edges of the side panels. Make sure the spreader will not interfere with door operation.

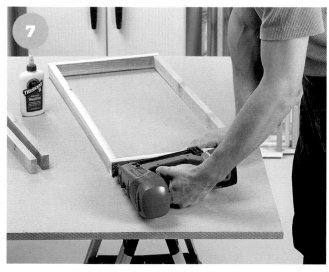

7 Make the grids for the panel infill areas. Use 1 × 2 cedar to make all parts. Use exterior glue and galvanized finish nails to connect the horizontal filler strips to the vertical infill pieces. Vary the heights and spacing of the filler for visual interest and to make the ends accessible for nailing.

8 Frame the grids with 1 × 2 strips cut to the correct length so each frame fits neatly inside a panel or door opening. Install the grid frames in the openings, making sure all front edges are flush.

continued

How to Build a Compost Bin (continued)

9 Attach the top rails that conceal the post tops and help tie the panels together. Attach the sides first using exterior glue and galvanized finish nails. Then, install the back rail on top of the side rails. Leave the front of the project open on top so you can load, unload, and turn over compost more easily.

10 Line the interior surfaces of the compost bin with ½" galvanized hardware cloth. Cut the hardware cloth to fit and fasten it with fence staples, galvanized U-nails, or narrow-crown pneumatic staples (⅝" minimum) driven every 6" or so. Make sure you don't leave any sharp edges protruding. Grind them down with a rotary tool or a file.

11 Set up the bin in your location. It should not be in direct contact with any structure. If you wish, apply a coat of exterior wood sealant to all wood surfaces—use a product that contains a UV inhibitor. **TIP:** Before setting up your compost bin, dig a hole just inside the area where the bin will be placed. This will increase you bin's capacity.

12 Add suitable organic matter to the bin and turn with a pitchfork occasionally to speed up the rate of aerobic decomposition. With a little nurturing and good conditions, a compost bin can yield several batches of usable compost in a growing season.

What to Compost, What Not to Compost

Vegetable plants soak up the materials that make up your compost, and these materials will play a vital role in the development of the vegetables that will grace your dinner table! When in doubt as to what should or shouldn't go into your compost pile for your garden, follow these general guidelines:

Great Garden Compost	Not for Compost, Please
"Clean" food scraps—including crushed eggshells, corncobs, vegetable scraps, oatmeal, stale bread, etc.	Fatty or greasy food scraps—including meat waste, bones, grease, dairy products, cooking oils, dressings, sandwich spreads, etc.
Vegetable and fruit peelings and leftovers	Fruit pits and seeds—These don't break down well and can attract rodents.
Coffee grounds and filters, tea leaves and tea bags	Metal. Remove the tea bag staples before composting!
Old potting soil	Diseased plant material
Lawn clippings	Weeds—These will only sprout in your garden! Kill the weed seeds and salvage the compostable bits by baking or microwaving the plants before adding them to your compost bin.
Prunings from your yard, chopped up in small pieces	Big chunks of yard debris or plants that are diseased or full of insect pests
Shredded leaves and pine needles	Any plant debris that has been treated with weed killer or pesticides
Shredded newspaper and telephone books—black and white pages only	Glossy color ads or wax-coated book covers
White or brown paper towels and napkins	Colored paper towels and napkins
Wood ash—use sparingly	Coal ash
Cardboard	Pizza boxes or other wax-coated food boxes
Livestock manure	Cat, dog, or other pet waste, which may contain meat products or parasites
Sawdust, wood chips, and woody brush	Sawdust from wood treated with preservatives
Straw or hay—the greener, the better!	
Wilted floral bouquets	

Raised Beds

Raised garden beds offer several advantages over planting at ground level. When segregated, soil can be amended in a more targeted way to support high density plantings. Also, in raised garden beds, soil doesn't suffer compaction from foot traffic or machinery, so plant roots are free to spread and breathe more easily. Vegetables planted at high densities in raised beds are placed far enough apart to avoid overcrowding, but close enough to shade and choke out weeds. In raised beds, you can also water plants easily with soaker hoses, which deliver water to soil and roots rather than spraying leaves and inviting disease. And if your plants develop a fungus or another disorder, it is easier to treat and less likely to migrate to other plants in a raised bed situation.

Raised garden beds can be built in a wide variety of shapes and sizes, and can easily be customized to fit the space you have available on your property. Just make sure you can reach the center easily. If you can only access your raised bed from one side, it's best to build it no wider than 3 ft. Beds that you can access from both sides can be as wide as 6 ft., as long as you can reach the center. You can build your raised bed as long as you'd like.

Raised garden beds can be built from a wide variety of materials: 2× lumber, 4 × 4 posts, salvaged timbers, even scrap metals and other recycled goods. Make sure any lumber you choose (either new or salvaged) hasn't been treated with creosote, pentachlorophenol,

> **TIP**
>
> **Bed Positions**
>
> If you're planting low-growing crops, position the bed with a north-south orientation, so both sides of the bed will be exposed to direct sunlight. For taller crops, position the bed east-west.

Raised garden beds make great vegetable gardens—they're easy to weed, simple to water, and the soil quality is easier to control, ensuring that your vegetable plants yield bountiful fresh produce. Your garden beds can be built at any height up to waist-level. It's best not to build them much taller than that, however, to make sure you can reach the center of your bed.

Vegetable Plant Compatibility Chart

Vegetable	Loves	Incompatible with	Planting Season
Asparagus	Tomatoes, parsley, basil		Early spring
Beans (bush)	Beets, carrots, cucumbers, potatoes	Fennel, garlic, onions	Spring
Cabbage & broccoli	Beets, celery, corn, dill, onions, oregano, sage	Fennel, pole beans, strawberries, tomatoes	Spring
Cantaloupe	Corn	Potatoes	Early summer
Carrots	Chives, leaf lettuce, onion, parsley, peas, rosemary, sage, tomatoes	Dill	Early spring
Celery	Beans, cabbages, cauliflower, leeks, tomatoes		Early summer
Corn	Beans, cucumbers, peas, potatoes, pumpkins, squash		Spring
Cucumbers	Beans, cabbages, corn, peas, radishes	Aromatic herbs, potatoes	Early summer
Eggplant	Beans	Potatoes	Spring
Lettuce	Carrots, cucumbers, onions, radishes, strawberries		Early spring
Onions & garlic	Beets, broccoli, cabbages, eggplant, lettuce, strawberries, tomatoes	Peas, beans	Early spring
Peas	Beans, carrots, corn, cucumbers, radishes, turnips	Chives, garlic, onions	Early spring
Potatoes	Beans, cabbage, corn, eggplant, peas	Cucumber, tomatoes, raspberries	Early spring
Pumpkins	Corn	Potatoes	Early summer
Radishes	Beans, beets, carrots, cucumbers, lettuce, peas, spinach, tomatoes		Early spring
Squash	Radishes	Potatoes	Early summer
Tomatoes	Asparagus, basil, carrots, chive, garlic, onions, parsley	Cabbages, fennel, potatoes	Dependent on the variety
Turnips	Beans, peas		Early spring

or chromated copper arsenic (CCA). Lumber treated with newer, non-arsenate chemicals at higher saturation levels is rated for ground contact and is also a safe choice for bed frames. Rot-resistant redwood and cedar are good choices that will stand the test of time. Other softwoods, including pine, tamarack, and cypress, will also work, but can be subject to rot and may need to be replaced after a few years.

Companion Planting

The old adage is true—some vegetables do actually get along "like peas and carrots." Some species of vegetables are natural partners that benefit from each other when planted close. On the other hand, some combinations are troublesome, and one plant will inhibit the growth of another. You can plant these antagonists in the same garden—even in the same raised garden bed—just don't place them side by side. Use the table on p. 34 to help you plan out your raised garden beds to ensure that your plants grow healthy, strong, and bear plentiful fruit.

Start with Healthy Soil

The success or failure of any gardening effort generally lies beneath the surface. Soil is the support system for all plants—it provides a balanced meal of the nutrients that plants' roots need to grow deep and strong. If you plan to fill your raised beds with soil from your property, it's a good idea to have the soil tested first to assess its quality. Take a sample of your soil and submit it to a local agricultural extension service—a basic lab test will cost you between $15 and $25 and will give you detailed information about the nutrients available in your property's soil. Mixing soil from your property with compost, potting soil, or other additives is a smart and inexpensive way to improve its quality. After you've filled your beds with soil, add a three-inch layer of mulch to the top to lock in moisture and keep your good soil from blowing away in strong winds. Lawn clippings, wood, or bark chips, hay and straw, leaves, compost, and shredded newspaper all work well as mulch materials.

Sprinklers with high, arching spray patterns are afflicted by excess water evaporation, but if you choose a small, controllable sprinkler with a water pattern that stays low to the ground you can deliver water to your raised bed with minimal loss.

> **TIP**
>
> **Watering Raised Beds**
>
> When the soil inside the planting bed pulls away from the edges of the bed, it's time to water. The best time of day to water is in the late afternoon or early- to mid-morning. Avoid watering in midday, when the sun is hottest and water will quickly evaporate, or near sundown or at night, when too much moisture in the soil can cause mold and fungus to grow.

How to Build a Raised Bed

1 This basic but very sturdy raised bed is made with 4 × 4 landscape timbers stacked with their ends staggered in classic log-cabin style. The corners are pinned together with 6" galvanized spikes (or, you can use timber screws). It is lined with landscape fabric and includes several weep holes in the bottom course for drainage. Consider adding a 2 × 8 ledge on the top row. Corner finials improve the appearance and provide hose guides to protect the plants in the bed.

2 Create an outline around your garden bed by tying mason's string to the stakes. Use a shovel to remove the grass inside the outline, then dig a 4"-wide trench for the first row of timbers around the perimeter. Lay the bottom course of timbers in the trenches. Where possible, add or remove soil as needed to bring the timbers to level—a level bed frame always looks better than a sloped one. If you do have a significant slope to address, terrace the beds.

3 Add the second layer, staggering the joints. Drill pilot holes at the corners and drive 6" galvanized spikes (or 6" to 8" timber screws) through the holes—use at least two per joint. Continue to build up layers in this fashion, until your bed reaches the desired height.

4 Line the bed with landscape fabric to contain the soil and help keep weeds out of the bed. Tack the fabric to the lower part of the top course with roofing nails. Some gardeners recommend drilling 1"-dia. weep holes in the bottom timber course at 2-ft. intervals. Fill with a blend of soil, peat moss, and fertilizer (if desired) to within 2 or 3" of the top.

How to Build a Raised Bed from a Kit

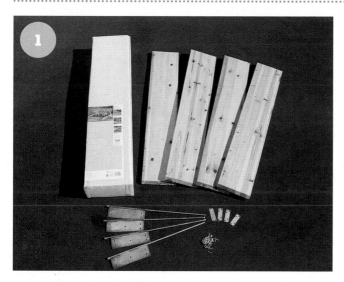

1 Raised garden bed kits come in many styles. Some have modular plastic or composite panels that fit together with grooves or with hardware. Others feature wood panels and metal corner hardware. Most kits can be stacked to increase bed height.

2 On a flat surface, assemble the panels and corner brackets (or hinge brackets) using the included hardware. Follow the kit instructions, making sure all corners are square.

3 Set the box down, experimenting with exact positioning until you find just the spot and angle you like. Be sure to observe the sun over an entire day when choosing the sunniest spot you can for growing vegetables. Cut around the edges of the planting bed box with a square-nose spade, move the box, and then slice off the sod in the bed area.

4 Set the bed box onto the installation site and check it for level. Add or remove soil as needed until it is level. Stake the box to the ground with the provided hardware. Add additional box kits on top of or next to the first box. Follow the manufacturer's instructions for connecting the modular units. Line the bed or beds with landscape fabric and fill with soil to within 2" or so of the top.

Container Gardening

If you're short on yard space but have a sunny spot like a balcony, stoop, porch, roof, or even windowsill, then you have the potential to plant a productive vegetable garden. Many plants flourish in small planters or other portable containers, and with a few well-managed containers, you can yield a sizable bounty for a couple or small family. In some ways, container gardening is easier than having a full-blown vegetable garden: There are fewer weeds (if any), pests are less problematic, and diseases are easier to avoid. You also need fewer tools and plants can easily be moved to accommodate temperature fluctuations and light/shade patterns. If you're a beginner gardener just wanting to try your hand at growing your own food, container gardening could be a great solution for you.

The key to successful container gardening is water. Because of their limited size, even the largest containers simply cannot hold the amount of water the plants need to thrive without watering once every day—extremely thirsty plants may even need to be watered more frequently than that. Vegetable plants are especially thirsty, but herbs and fruit

TIP

Fresh Soil

Do not reuse soil if you're growing tomatoes or other plants that are susceptible to blight and fungus. After the growing season is concluded, collect the soil from sensitive plant containers and disperse it into hardy planting beds.

If you've never tried gardening, container gardening is a good way to start.

What to Grow

Most plants that grow well in your garden will also thrive in containers. Root vegetables are perhaps the only exception to this rule. Keep in mind that the larger the plant, the larger the container you'll need. Generally, the plant should not be more than twice the height of the pot or 1½ times as wide. Use the guidelines below as a rough guide.

Containers 4 to 6" deep: Mustard greens, radishes, and spinach can all grow in shallow containers.

Containers at least 8" deep: Corn (container must be at least 21" wide, however, and house at least three plants to assure pollination), kale, lettuce.

Containers at least 12" deep: Beans, beets, brussel sprouts, cabbage (should also be pretty wide), carrots, chard, collards, kohlrabi, onion, peas, turnips, zucchini.

Containers at least 16" deep: Cucumber, eggplant, peppers.

Containers at least 20" deep: Broccoli, bok choy, Chinese cabbage.

More than 24" deep: Squash, tomatoes.

trees or bushes need careful watering as well. Mature tomato plants may need as much as a gallon of water every day to grow those juicy, delicious fruits. If you bury your finger in the pot and you feel any dry soil—even 2" down—it's time to water.

Soil in container gardens is important too. A reliable rule of thumb is to use a 50/50 mix of potting soil to compost. Soil from your property typically won't hold water as well as potting soil on its own, so it's best not to use it in container gardens without adding a significant amount of organic fertilizer, which you can buy at the garden center or mix yourself. The following pages provide guidelines about the types of containers you can use and step-by-step instructions to help you build your own planter boxes.

○ Container Types and Recommendations

As a container gardener, you'll quickly discover that the universe of usable containers is infinitely larger than the plain clay flowerpot. Essentially, any sturdy, watertight container will do. Large containers like wine barrels or old wash tubs and smaller containers like an ice cream pail or 5-gallon bucket can all be good for different kinds of plants. Large wooden troughs and DIY planter boxes can be customized to your garden (and are fun to make, too). When building your own planters, it's a good idea to line the inside with perforated polyethylene sheeting before adding potting soil to protect the wood from rot and to make it easier to empty out soil after a season.

Always make sure that the container you choose did not previously hold any kind of chemical and, if it does not already have them, drill drainage holes near the bottom of the container before filling with soil. If you'll be using large containers, it's usually a good idea to place them on a platform fitted with casters before filling them with potting soil.

Self-watering pots make container gardening less of a drain on your time. These containers are, essentially, a flowerpot set just above a reservoir of water. With this type of container, the soil above will wick up moisture from the reservoir as it needs it—keeping the soil consistently moist throughout and eliminating the possibility of over-watering. With a self-watering container, you may only need to add water every three to four days, and your plants will likely be less stressed. Ideally, your plants will therefore provide a more sizable crop at the end of the season.

Spinach, leaf lettuce and a few shallots co-exist in this self-watering planter. Self-watering containers have a water reservoir below to keep the soil in the pot moist. All you have to do is keep the reservoir full, and rainfall may even take care of this for you.

Many varieties of vegetables and fruits can be grown in pots, planters, and other vessels—just make sure to select a container that is the right size for your plant and always add ample drainage holes if they're not already present.

○ Planter Boxes

Decorating a garden is much like decorating a room in your home—it's nice to have pieces that are adaptable enough that you can move them around occasionally and create a completely new look. After all, most of us can't buy new furniture every time we get tired of the way our living rooms look. And we can't build or buy new garden furnishings every time we want to rearrange the garden.

That's one of the reasons this trio of planter boxes works so well. In addition to being handsome—especially when flowers are bursting out of them—they're incredibly adaptable. You can follow these plans to build a terrific trio of planter boxes that will go well with each other and will complement most gardens, patios, and decks. Or you can tailor the plans to suit your needs. For instance, you may want three boxes that are exactly the same size. Or you might want to build several more and use them as a border that encloses a patio or frames a terraced area.

Whatever the dimensions of the boxes, the basic construction steps are the same. If you decide to alter the designs, take a little time to figure out the new dimensions and sketch plans. Then devise a new cutting list and do some planning so you can make efficient use of materials. To save cutting time, clamp together parts that are the same size and shape and cut them as a group (called gang cutting).

When your planter boxes have worn out their welcome in one spot, you can easily move them to another, perhaps with a fresh coat of stain, and add new plantings. You can even use the taller boxes to showcase outdoor relief sculptures—a kind of alfresco sculpture gallery.

Whether you build only one or all three, these handy cedar planters are small enough to move around your gardens and inside your greenhouse or garden shed.

Building Planter Boxes

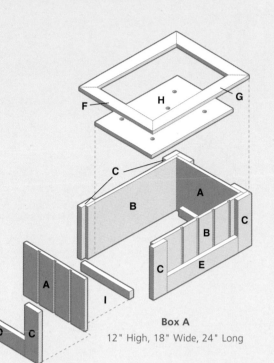

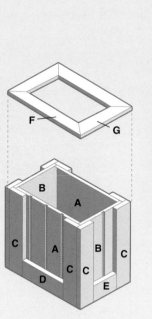

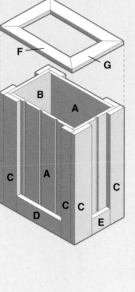

Box A
12" High, 18" Wide, 24" Long

Box B
18" High, 18" Wide, 12" Long

Box C
24" High, 18" Wide, 12" Long

CUTTING LIST

Key	No.	Part	Box A Dimension	Box B Dimension	Box C Dimension	Material
A	2	End panel	⅝ × 15 × 11⅛"	⅝ × 15 × 17⅛"	⅝ × 15 × 23⅛"	Siding
B	2	Side panel	⅝ × 22¼ × 11⅛"	⅝ × 10¼ × 17⅛"	⅝ × 10¼ × 23⅛"	Siding
C	8	Corner trim	⅞ × 3½ × 11⅛"	⅞ × 3½ × 17⅛"	⅞ × 3½ × 23⅛"	Cedar
D	2	Bottom trim	⅞ × 3½ × 9¼"	⅞ × 3½ × 9¼"	⅞ × 3½ × 9¼"	Cedar
E	2	Bottom trim	⅞ × 3½ × 17"	⅞ × 3½ × 5"	⅞ × 3½ × 5"	Cedar
F	2	Top cap	⅞ × 1½ × 18"	⅞ × 1½ × 18"	⅞ × 1½ × 18"	Cedar
G	2	Top cap	⅞ × 1½ × 24"	⅞ × 1½ × 12"	⅞ × 1½ × 12"	Cedar
H	1	Bottom panel	¾ × 14½ × 19½"	¾ × 14½ × 8½"	¾ × 14½ × 8½"	Plywood
I	2	Cleat	⅞ × 1½ × 12"	⅞ × 1½ × 12"	⅞ × 1½ × 12"	Cedar

Note: Measurements reflect the actual size of dimension lumber.

TOOLS AND MATERIALS

Tape measure
Circular saw
Straightedge
Drill
Finishing sander

Miter box and backsaw
(3) 8-ft. cedar 1 × 2s
(6) 8-ft. cedar 1 × 4s
4 × 8-ft. sheet of ⅝" T1-11 siding
2 × 4-ft. piece ¾" CDX plywood

1¼" galvanized deck screws
1⅝" galvanized deck screws
6d galvanized finish nails
Exterior wood stain
Paintbrush

Landscape fabric

How to Build Planter Boxes

1 Cut all the wood parts to size according to the Cutting List on page 43. Use a circular saw and a straightedge cutting guide to rip siding panels (if you have access to a tablesaw, use that instead). You can make all three sizes, or any combination you choose.

2 Assemble the box frame. Place the end panel face down and butt it against a side panel. Mark the locations of several fasteners on the side panel. Drill counterbored $3/32$" pilot holes in the side panel at the marked locations and fasten the side panel to the end panel with $1 5/8$" deck screws. Fasten the opposite side panel the same way. Attach the other end panel with deck screws.

3 Attach the corner trim. Position one piece of corner trim flush to the corner edge and fasten to the panels with $1 5/8$" galvanized deck screws driven into the trim from the inside of the box. Place the second piece of trim flush to the edge of the first piece, creating a square butt joint. Attach to the panel with $1 5/8$" galvanized deck screws. For extra support, end nail the two trim pieces together at the corner with galvanized finish nails.

4 Attach the bottom trim. Fasten the bottom trim to the end and side panels, between the corner trim pieces and flush with the bottom of the box. Drive $1 1/4$" deck screws through the panels from the inside to fasten the trim pieces to the box.

5 Attach the cap pieces. Cut 45° miters at both ends of one cap piece using a miter box and backsaw or a power miter saw. Tack this piece to the top end of the box, with the outside edges flush with the outer edges of the corner trim. Miter both ends of each piece and tack to the box to make a square corner with the previously installed piece. Once all caps are tacked in position and the miters are closed cleanly, attach the cap pieces using 6d galvanized finish nails.

6 Install the cleats to hold the box bottom in place. Screw to the inside of the end panels with 1⅝" deck screws. If your planter is extremely tall, fasten the cleats higher on the panels so you won't need as much soil to fill the box. If doing so, add cleats on the side panels as well for extra support.

7 Finish and install the bottom. Cut the bottom panel to size from ¾"-thick exterior-rated plywood. Drill several 1"-dia. drainage holes in the panel and set it onto the cleats. The bottom panel does not need to be fastened in place, but for extra strength, nail it to the cleats and box sides with galvanized finish nails.

8 Finish the box or boxes with wood sealer-preservative. When the finish has dried, line the planter box with landscape fabric, stapling it at the top of the box. Trim off fabric at least a couple of inches below the top of the box. Add a 2"-layer of gravel or stones, then fill with a 50/50 mix of potting soil and compost. **TIP:** Add wheels or casters to your planter boxes before filling them with soil. Be sure to use locking wheels or casters with brass or plastic housings.

○ Building an Old-fashioned Strawberry Barrel

Container gardens aren't just for vegetables—fruit trees and berry bushes also thrive in a potted garden environment and can produce enough fruit for a family to enjoy throughout the summer. Strawberries, which typically grow in long rows or patches in the ground, can also be grown in a converted barrel. Two can be enough space to grow the equivalent of 25 feet of strawberry plants. For this project, make sure you choose everbearing strawberry varieties, and cut off runners for transplanting when they appear. Insulate your barrels with hay or straw during the winter, and you can enjoy a strawberry crop for several years. To keep your barrel going, start fresh every four or five years with new plants and new soil.

TOOLS & MATERIALS

Large, clean barrel (55-gallon plastic or wood)

Pry bar or jigsaw

3"-dia. hole saw

Drill

4"-dia. PVC Pipe

Window screen or hardware cloth

Gravel

Potting soil mix

Strawberry plants

A strawberry barrel planter can grow the equivalent of 25 ft. of strawberry plants; choose everbearing varieties for best results.

How to Build a Strawberry Barrel

1 Prepare the barrel. If your barrel has a lid or closed top, remove it with a pry bar. If your barrel does not have a lid, cut a large opening in the top with a jigsaw. Beginning about 1 ft. above the ground, use a hole saw to cut 3"-dia. planting holes around the barrel, about 10" apart. Stagger the holes diagonally in each row and space the rows about 10" apart. Leave at least 12" above the top row of holes. Flip the barrel over and drill about a half dozen ½"-dia. drainage holes in the bottom.

2 Prepare the watering pipe. Cut a section of 4"-dia. PVC pipe to fit inside the barrel from top to bottom. Punch or drill ¾"-dia. holes in the pipe every 4 to 6", all the way around. Cut a section of window screen or hardware cloth to fit inside the bottom of the barrel and place it inside. Cover the screen with 2" of gravel or small rocks.

3 Begin to fill the barrel with soil. Have a friend hold the watering pipe in the center of the barrel and fill the pipe with coarse gravel. Then, begin to add soil to the bottom of the barrel, packing it firmly around the watering pipe in the bottom with a piece of scrap lumber. Add water to help the soil settle. Continuing adding soil until you reach the bottom of your first row of planting holes.

4 Add soil and plants. Carefully insert your strawberry plants into the holes, spreading the roots into a fan shape. Add soil on top of the roots and lightly water. Continue to add soil and plants, packing soil gently and watering after each planting, until you reach the top of the barrel. Do not cover the watering pipe. Plant additional strawberries on top of the barrel. Insert a hose into the watering pipe and run water for several minutes to give the barrel a good soaking.

Building a Cold Frame

An inexpensive foray into greenhouse gardening, a cold frame is practical for starting plants six to eight weeks earlier in the growing season and for hardening off seedlings. Basically, a cold frame is a box set on the ground and topped with glass or plastic. Although mechanized models with thermostatically controlled atmospheres and sash that automatically open and close are available, you can easily build a basic cold frame yourself from materials you probably already have around the house.

The back of the frame should be about twice as tall as the front so the lid slopes to a favorable angle for capturing sunrays. Build the frame tall enough to accommodate the maximum height of the plants before they are removed. The frame can be made of brick, block, plastic, wood, or just about any material you have on hand. It should be built to keep drafts out and soil in.

If the frame is permanently sited, position it facing south to receive maximum light during winter and spring and to offer protection from wind. Partially burying it takes advantage of the insulation from the earth, but it also can cause water to collect and the direct soil contact will shorten the lifespan of the wood frame parts. Locating your frame near a wall, rock, or building adds additional insulation and protection from the elements. **TIP:** The ideal temperature inside is 65 to 75° F during the day and 55 to 65° at night. Keep an inexpensive thermometer in a shaded spot inside the frame for quick

Starting plants early in a cold frame is a great way to get a head start on the growing season. A cold frame is also a great place for hardening off delicate seedlings to prepare them for transplanting.

reference. A bright spring day can heat a cold frame to as warm as 100°, so prop up or remove the cover as necessary to prevent overheating. And remember, the more you vent, the more you should water. On cold nights, especially when frost is predicted, cover the box with burlap, old quilts, or leaves to keep it warm inside.

A cold frame should only be used during the early, cooler days of the growing season when delicate seedlings need that extra protection, and for late-season frost protection. Once the warmer weather arrives and the plants are established, remove and relocate the cold frame. Ongoing usage will overheat and kill the plants. And while the clear acrylic lid on this cold frame is desirable because it is safer to work with and use than glass, too much heat buildup can cause the acrylic to warp.

Building a Cold Frame

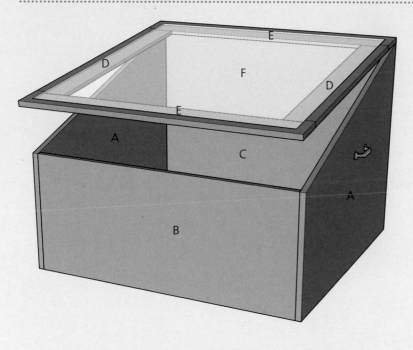

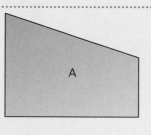

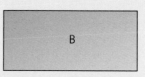

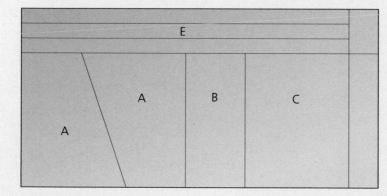

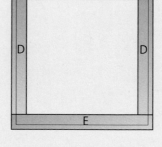

CUTTING LIST

Key	Part	No.	Size	Material
A	Side	2	¾ x 16/28 x 36"	Ext. Plywood
B	Front	1	¾ x 16 x 36"	Ext. Plywood
C	Back	1	¾ x 28 x 36"	Ext. Plywood
D	Lid frame	2	¾ x 4 x 31"	Ext. Plywood
E	Lid frame	2	¾ x 4 x 38"	Ext. Plywood
F	Cover	1	⅛ x 37 x 38"	Plexiglas

TOOLS AND MATERIALS

(2) 3 x 3" butt hinges (ext.)	Exterior paint
(2) 4" utility handles	2" deck screws
(4) Corner L-brackets (¾ x 2½")	#8 x ¾" wood screws
(1) ¾" x 4 x 8 ft. Plywood (Ext.)	Circular saw
⅛ x 37 x 38" clear Plexiglas	Drill/driver
Exterior caulk/adhesive	Pipe clamps
Exterior wood glue	Straightedge cutting guide

How to Build a Plywood Cold Frame

1 Cut the parts. This project, as dimensioned, is designed to be made entirely from a single 4 × 8 sheet of plywood. Start by cutting the plywood lengthwise to make a 36"-wide piece. **TIP:** Remove material in 4" wide strips and use the strips to make the lid frame parts and any other trim you may want to add.

2 Trim the parts to size with a circular saw or jigsaw and cutting guide. Mark the cutting lines first (See Diagram, p. 51).

3 Assemble the front, back, and side panels into a square box. Glue the joints and clamp them together with pipe or bar clamps. Adjust until the corners are square.

4 Reinforce the joints with 2" deck screws driven through countersunk pilot holes. Drive a screw every 4 to 6" along each joint.

5 Make the lid frame. Cut the 4"-wide strips of ¾" plywood reserved from step 1 into frame parts. Assemble the frame parts into a square 38 × 39" frame. There are many ways to join the parts so they create a flat frame. Because the Plexiglas cover will give the lid some rigidity, simply gluing the joints and reinforcing with an L-bracket at each inside corner is adequate structurally.

6 Paint the box and the frame with exterior paint, preferably in an enamel finish. A darker color will hold more solar heat.

7 Lay thick beads of clear exterior adhesive/caulk onto the tops of the frames and then seat the Plexiglas cover into the adhesive. Clean up squeeze-out right away. Once the adhesive has set, attach the lid with butt hinges and attach the handles to the sides.

8 Move the cold frame to the site. Clear and level the ground where it will set. Some gardeners like to excavate the site slightly—see discussion on page 49.

Starting & Transplanting Seedlings

Add weeks to your garden's growing season by starting seeds indoors, then transplanting them to the garden after the danger of frost is past. Seedlings are available for purchase at the garden center in the spring, of course, but starting your own at home presents a number of advantages:

- Buying seeds is less expensive than buying seedlings.

- You can cull out all but the strongest seedlings, which will hopefully result in stronger plants and a more bountiful crop.

- Garden centers sell seeds for a diverse and varied array of plants, but seedlings for only the most common species. Seed catalogs introduce an entirely new selection as well.

- You can be certain that unwanted pesticides have not been used on the plants in your garden, even in their infancy.

Start your seeds eight to ten weeks before you plan to transplant them into your garden. To get started, you'll need a few small containers, a suitable growing medium, and a bright spot for the seedlings to grow—either a sunny window that receives at least six hours of bright sunlight per day, a greenhouse, or a planting table in your home that's

Using colored cups as starter containers has the advantage of letting you color-code your plants so you can avoid any confusion. Beginning gardeners often have trouble distinguishing one pot from another when they are still seedlings. Here, the red cups clearly communicate "tomato."

Seedlings need a lot of water, sunlight, and warmth in their infancy. A kitchen window or greenhouse is an ideal growing environment for propagating plants.

55

illuminated by artificial grow lights. If you're planning to raise your seedlings by artificial light, position one or two fluorescent lighting fixtures fitted with 40-watt, full-spectrum bulbs about six inches above the seedlings. Leave fluorescent lights on for 12 to 16 hours a day—many gardeners find it helpful to connect the fixture to a timer to ensure their plants receive adequate light each day.

A 4-ft., two-bulb fluorescent light fixture that can be raised or lowered over a table is really all you need to start your vegetable plants indoors.

Growing Mediums

If you plan to use your own garden soil or compost, prepare your seedling containers in the fall, before the ground gets too cold and wet.

Almost any small container can be used to grow seedlings. Just make sure the container you use is clean and hasn't had contact with any chemical that could be poisonous to plants. Also, remember to cut a drainage hole in the bottom of your container before filling it with soil. Drainage is very important to ensure that your plants are well ventilated. Excessively moist soil can result in mold or other diseases, as well. Good options for seedling containers include:

- Peat pots or pellets
- Fiber cubes
- Used plastic jugs
- Cans (any size)
- Used plastic tubs (i.e., sour cream,
- cottage cheese, or margarine containers)
- Used yogurt cups
- Egg cartons
- Small paper cups

○ Starting Seedlings

1. **Planting:** Sow three to four seeds in each container according to the instructions on the seed packet—as a general rule, large seeds should be buried and small seeds can be sprinkled on top of the soil. Label the container with the type of plant and the date your seeds were planted.

2. **Germination:** Water the seeds whenever the containers look dry. Until the seeds sprout, keep seedlings in a dark, warm space. Cover germinating seeds with plastic bags or plastic wrap. Open the plastic for a few hours every few days to let the soil breathe, then re-close.

3. **Sprouts:** When the seeds sprout, remove plastic covering and move them into direct light. Seedlings need lots of light to grow. Keep the soil medium moist but not soggy. Remember, multiple light waterings are better for seedlings than the occasional soaking.

4. **Culling:** When the true leaves appear (see illustration), cut off all but the strongest seedling in each container at soil level. Do not pull up the unwanted seedlings, as this may damage the roots of the seedling you're cultivating. You may also choose to fertilize every week or so as your seedlings grow.

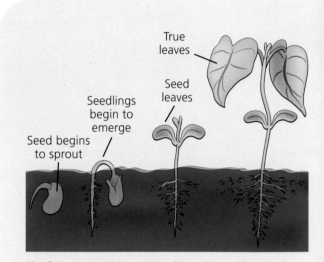

The four stages in the growth of a seedling are illustrated above. Note that seed leaves and true leaves serve different purposes and will look different. When a plant has 4 to 8 true leaves, it is ready for transplanting.

○ Hardening Off and Transplanting

When your seedlings have four to eight true leaves, they should be hardened off, then transplanted to the garden. Hardening off is the process of gradually introducing the plant to outdoor conditions so it is not shocked when you move it outside permanently. About two weeks before planting, place your seedlings outdoors for an hour the first day, and then gradually increase the time until your seedlings spend the whole day outside. Protect seedlings from wind and do not expose them to the midday sun for the first few days. Stop fertilizing seedlings during the last week. A cold frame is a great environment for hardening off seedlings. Seedlings can stay in a cold frame for two to three weeks, gradually getting used to the cooler air and chilly nights before they go out into the garden. Open the lid of the cold frame a little bit more each day.

Transplant your seedlings into the garden on a cloudy day or in late afternoon to avoid excessive drying from the sun. Remove seedlings gently from their containers, holding as much soil as possible around the roots (containers that are pressed from peat are not intended to be removed). Place each into a hole in your garden, spreading the roots carefully, then pack soil around the seedling to hold it straight and strong. Thoroughly soak all seedlings with a very gentle water spray after they've been planted. If you have a rain barrel or another source for untreated water, this is a perfect application for it: The chlorine in most municipal water can be harmful to delicate plants.

Building a Greenhouse

Utilizing a greenhouse is a great way to extend and diversify your garden, enabling you to grow more food for a longer period of time—and perhaps even grow foods that wouldn't otherwise survive in your climate. A greenhouse can be a decorative and functional building that adds beauty to your property, or a quick and easy temporary structure that serves a purpose and then disappears. The wood-framed greenhouse in this project is somewhere between these two types. The sturdy wood construction will hold up for many seasons. The plastic sheeting covering will last one to five seasons, depending on the material you choose, and is easy to replace when it starts to degrade.

The five-foot-high kneewalls in this design provide ample space for installing and working on a conventional-height potting table. For a door, this plan simply employs a sheet of weighted plastic that can be tied out of the way for entry and exit. If you plan to go in and out frequently, you can purchase a prefabricated greenhouse door from a garden center or greenhouse materials provider. To allow for ventilation in hot weather, we built a wood-frame vent cover that fits over one rafter bay and can be propped open easily.

A wood-frame greenhouse with sheet-plastic cover is an inexpensive, semipermanent gardening structure that can be used as a potting area as well as a protective greenhouse.

Where to Site Your Greenhouse

When the first orangeries (early greenhouses) were built, heat was thought to be the most important element for successfully growing plants indoors. Most orangeries had solid roofs and walls with large windows. Once designers realized that light was more important than heat for plant growth, they began to build greenhouses from glass.

All plants need at least six (and preferably 12) hours of light a day year-round, so when choosing a site for a greenhouse, you need to consider a number of variables. Be sure that it is clear of shadows cast by trees, hedges, fences, your house, and other buildings. Don't forget that the shade cast by obstacles changes throughout the year. Take note of the sun's position at various times of the year: A site that receives full sun in the spring and summer can be shaded by nearby trees when the sun is low in winter. Winter shadows are longer than those cast by the high summer sun, and during winter, sunlight is particularly important for keeping the greenhouse warm. If you are not familiar with the year-round sunlight patterns on your property, you may have to do a little geometry to figure out where shadows will fall. Your latitude will also have a bearing on the amount of sunlight available; greenhouses at northern latitudes receive fewer hours of winter sunlight than those located farther south. You may have to supplement natural light with interior lighting.

To gain the most sun exposure, the greenhouse should be oriented so that its ridge runs east to west (see illustration), with the long sides facing north and south. A slightly southwest or southeast exposure is also acceptable, but avoid a northern exposure if you're planning an attached greenhouse; only shade-lovers will grow there.

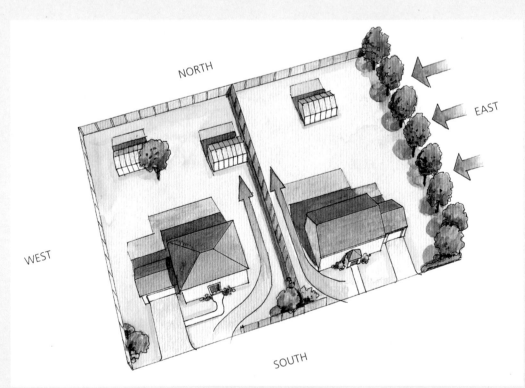

The ideal greenhouse location is well away from trees but protected from prevailing winds, usually by another structure, a fence or a wall.

For maximum heat gain, orient your greenhouse so the roof or wall with the most surface area is as close to perpendicular to the sunrays as it can be.

Building a Greenhouse

CUTTING LIST

Key	No.	Part	Dimension	Material
A	2	Base ends	3½ x 3½ x 96"	4 x 4 landscape timber
B	2	Base sides	3½ x 3½ x 113"	4 x 4 landscape timber
C	2	Sole plates end	1½ x 3½ x 89"	2 x 4 pressure treated
D	2	Sole plates side	1½ x 3½ x 120"	2 x 4 pressure treated
E	12	Wall studs side	1½ x 3½ x 57"	2 x 4
F	1	Ridge support	1½ x 3½ x 91"	2 x 4
G	2	Back studs	1½ x 3½ x 76" *	2 x 4
H	2	Door frame sides	1½ x 3½ x 81" *	2 x 4
I	1	Cripple stud	1½ x 3½ x 16"	2 x 4
J	1	Door header	1½ x 3½ x 32"	2 x 4
K	2	Kneewall caps	1½ x 3½ x 120"	2 x 4
L	1	Ridge pole	1½ x 3½ x 120"	2 x 4
M	12	Rafters	1½ x 3½ x 60" *	2 x 4

*Approximate dimension; take actual length and angle measurements on structure before cutting.

TOOLS & MATERIALS

(1) 20 x 50-ft. roll 4 or 6-mil polyethylene sheeting or greenhouse fabric, tack strips

(12) 24"-long pieces of No. 3 rebar

(4) 16-ft. pressure-treated 2 x 4

(2) exterior-rated butt hinges

(1) screw-eye latch

(8) 8" timber screws

Reciprocating saw

Level

Carpenter's square

Drill with a nut driver bit

Eye and ear protection

Metal cutoff saw

Maul or sledgehammer

Speed square

3" deck screws

Exterior panel adhesive

Caulk gun

Hammer

Jigsaw or handsaw

Miter saw

Circular saw

Utility knife

Pneumatic nailer

Scissors

Scrap 2x4

Pencil

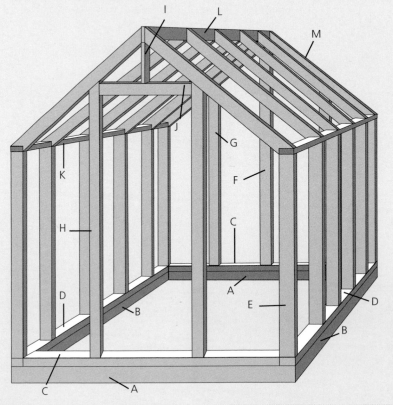

How to Build a Gabled Greenhouse

1 Prepare the installation area so it is flat and well drained; then cut the base timbers (4 × 4 landscape timbers) to length. Arrange the timbers so they are flat and level and create a rectangle with square corners. Drive a pair of 8" timber screws at each corner, using a drill/driver with a nut-driver bit.

2 Cut 12 pieces of No. 3 rebar (find it in the concrete supplies section of any building center) to 24" in length to use as spikes for securing the timbers to the ground. A metal cutoff saw or a reciprocating saw with a metal cutting blade can be used to make the cuts. Drill a ⅜" guide hole through each timber near each end and in the middle. Drive a rebar spike at each hole with a maul or sledgehammer until the top is flush with the wood.

3 Cut the plates and studs for the two side walls (called knee-walls). Arrange the parts on a flat surface and assemble the walls by driving three 3" deck screws through the cap and base plates and into the ends of the studs. Make both kneewalls.

continued

How to Build a Gabled Greenhouse (continued)

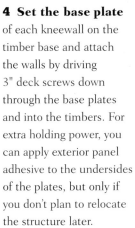

4 Set the base plate of each kneewall on the timber base and attach the walls by driving 3" deck screws down through the base plates and into the timbers. For extra holding power, you can apply exterior panel adhesive to the undersides of the plates, but only if you don't plan to relocate the structure later.

Temporary post

Ridge pole

5 Cut the ridge support post to length and attach it to the center of one end base plate, forming a T. Cut another post the same length for the front (this will be a temporary post) and attach it to a plate. Fasten both plates to front and back end timbers.

6 Set the ridge pole on top of the posts and check that it is level. Also check that the posts are level and plumb. Attach a 2 × 4 brace to the outer studs of the kneewalls and to the posts to hold them in square relationship. Double-check the pole and posts with the level.

7 Cut a 2 x 4 to about 66" to use as a rafter template. Hold the 2 × 4 against the end of the ridge pole and the top outside corner of a kneewall. Trace along the face of the ridge and the top plate of the wall to mark cutting lines. Cut the rafter and use it as a template for the other rafters on that side of the roof. Create a separate template for the other side of the roof.

8 Mark cutting lines for the rafters using the templates, and cut them all. You'll need to use a jigsaw or handsaw to make the bird's mouth cuts on the rafter ends that rest on the kneewall.

9 Attach the rafters to the ridge pole and the kneewalls with deck screws driven through pilot holes. Try to make the rafters align with the kneewall studs.

continued

How to Build a Gabled Greenhouse (continued)

10 Mark the positions for the remaining end wall studs on the base plate. At each location, hold a 2 × 4 on end on the base plate and make it level and plumb. Trace a cutting line at the top of the 2 × 4 where it meets the rafter. Cut the studs and install them by driving screws toenail-style.

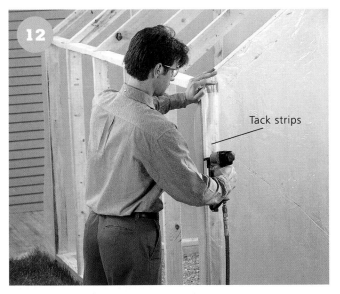

Tack strips

11 Measure up 78" (or less if you want a shorter door) from the sole plate in the door opening and mark a cutting line on the temporary ridge post. Make a square cut along the line with a circular saw or cordless trim saw (inset). Then cut the door header to fit between the vertical door frame members. Screw the header to the cut end of the ridge post and drive screws through the frame members and into the header.

12 Begin covering the greenhouse with your choice of cover material. (We used 6-mil polyethylene sheeting.) Start at the ends. Cut the sheeting to size and then fasten it by attaching screen retainer strips to wood surfaces at the edges of the area being covered. Tack the sheeting first at the top, then at the sides and finally at the bottom. After the strips are installed (use wire brads), trim the sheeting along the edges of the strips with a utility knife.

13 Attach the sheeting to the outside edge of the base plate on one side. Roll sheeting over the roof and down the other side. Draw it taut and cut it slightly overlong with scissors. Attach retainer strips to the other base plate and then to the outside edges of the corner studs.

14 Make and hang a door. We simply cut a piece of sheet plastic a little bigger than the opening (32") and hung it with retainer strips from the header. Attach a piece of 2 × 4 to the bottom of the door for weight.

15 *Option:* Make a vent window. First, cut a hole in the roof in one rafter bay and tack the cut edges of the plastic to the faces (not the edges) of the rafters, ridge pole, and wall cap. Then build a frame from 1 × 2 stock that will span from the ridge to the top of the kneewall and extend a couple of inches past the rafters at the side of the opening. Clad the frame with plastic sheeting and attach it to the ridge pole with butt hinges. Install a screw-eye latch to secure it at the bottom. Make and attach props if you wish.

Building a Hoophouse

The hoophouse is a popular garden structure for two main reasons: It is cheap to build and easy to build. In many agricultural areas you will see hoophouses snaking across vast fields of seedlings, protecting the delicate plants at their most vulnerable stages. Because they are portable and easy to disassemble, they can be removed when the plants are established and less vulnerable.

While hoophouses are not intended as inexpensive substitutes for real greenhouses, they do serve an important agricultural purpose. And building your own is a fun project that the whole family can enjoy.

The hoophouse shown here is essentially a Quonset-style frame of bent ¾" PVC tubing draped with sheet plastic. Each semicircular frame is actually made from two 10-ft. lengths of tubing that fit into a plastic fitting at the apex of the curve. PVC tubes tend to stay together simply by friction-fitting into the fittings, so you don't normally need to solvent glue the connections (this is important to the easy-to-disassemble and store feature). If you experience problems with the frame connections separating, try cutting 4" to 6"-long pieces of ½" (outside diameter) PVC tubing and inserting them into the tubes and fittings like splines. This will stiffen the connections.

A hoophouse is a temporary agricultural structure designed to be low-cost and portable. Also called Quonset houses and tunnel houses, hoophouses provide shelter and shade (depending on the film you use) and protection from wind and the elements. They will boost heat during the day, but are less efficient than paneled greenhouses for extending the growing season.

Hoophouse frames can be made from wood instead of PVC plastic. Wood allows you to attach plastic sheeting with retainer strips and staples.

Building & Siting a Hoophouse

The fact that a hoophouse is a temporary structure doesn't give you license to skimp on the construction. When you consider how light the parts are and how many properties sheet plastic shares with boat sails, the importance of securely anchoring your hoophouse becomes obvious. Use long stakes (at least 24") to anchor the tubular frames, and make sure you have plenty of excess sheeting at the sides of the hoophouse so the cover can be held down with ballast. Creating pockets at the ends of the sheeting and inserting scrap lumber is the ballasting technique shown here, but it is also common (especially when building in a field) to weigh down the sheeting by burying the ends in dirt. Only attach the sheeting at the ends of the tubular frame, and where possible, orient the structure so the prevailing winds won't blow through the tunnel.

TIP

Building a Hoophouse

- Space frame hoops about 3 ft. apart.

- Leave ridge members a fraction of an inch (not more than ¼") shorter than the span, which will cause the structure to be slightly shorter on top than at the base. This helps stabilize the structure.

- Orient the structure so the wall faces into the prevailing wind rather than the end openings.

- If you are using long-lasting greenhouse fabric for the cover, protect the investment by spray-painting the frame hoops with primer so there is no plastic-to-plastic contact.

- Because hoophouses are temporary structures that are designed to be disassembled or moved regularly, you do not need to include a base.

- The ¾" PVC pipes used to make the hoop frames are sold in 10 ft. lengths. Two pipes fitted into a tee or cross fitting at the top will result in legs that are 10 ft. apart at the base and a ridge that is roughly 7 ft. tall.

- Clip the hoophouse covers to the end frames. Clips fastened at the intermediate hoops will either fly off or tear the plastic cover in windy conditions.

Row tunnels are often used in vegetable gardens to protect sensitive plants in the spring and fall. Plastic or fabric sheeting is draped over a short wire or plastic framework to protect plants at night. During the heat of the day, the sheeting can be drawn back to allow plants direct sunlight.

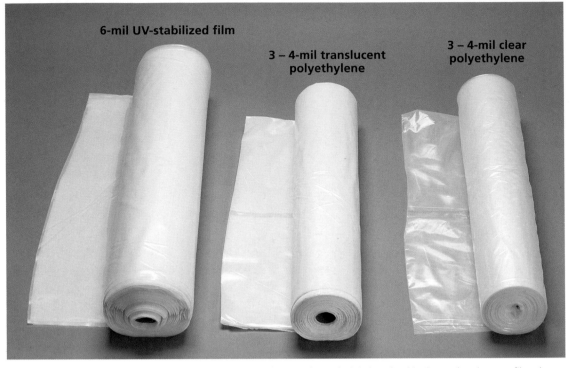

6-mil UV-stabilized film

3 – 4-mil translucent polyethylene

3 – 4-mil clear polyethylene

Sheet plastic is an inexpensive material for creating a greenhouse. Obviously, it is less durable than polycarbonate, fiberglass, or glass panels. But UV-stabilized films at least 6-mil thick can be rated to withstand four years or more of exposure. Inexpensive polyethylene sheeting (the kind you find at hardware stores) will hold up for a year or two, but it becomes brittle when exposed to sunlight. Some greenhouse builders prefer to use clear plastic sheeting to maximize the sunlight penetration, but the cloudiness of translucent poly makes it effective for diffusing light and preventing overheating. For the highest quality film coverings, look for film rated for greenhouse and agricultural use.

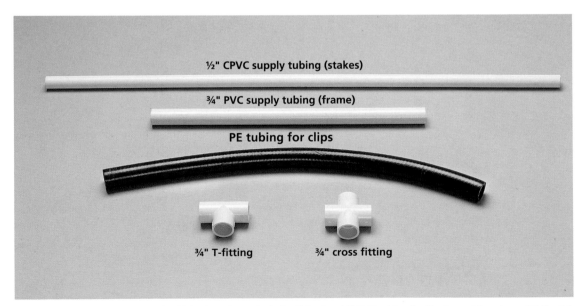

½" CPVC supply tubing (stakes)

¾" PVC supply tubing (frame)

PE tubing for clips

¾" T-fitting

¾" cross fitting

Plastic tubing and fittings used to build this hoophouse include: Light duty ¾" PVC tubing for the frame (do not use CPVC—it is too rigid and won't bend properly); ½" CPVC supply tubing for the frame stakes (rigidity is good here); Polyethylene (PE) tubing for the cover clips; T-fittings and cross fittings to join the frame members.

Building a Hoophouse

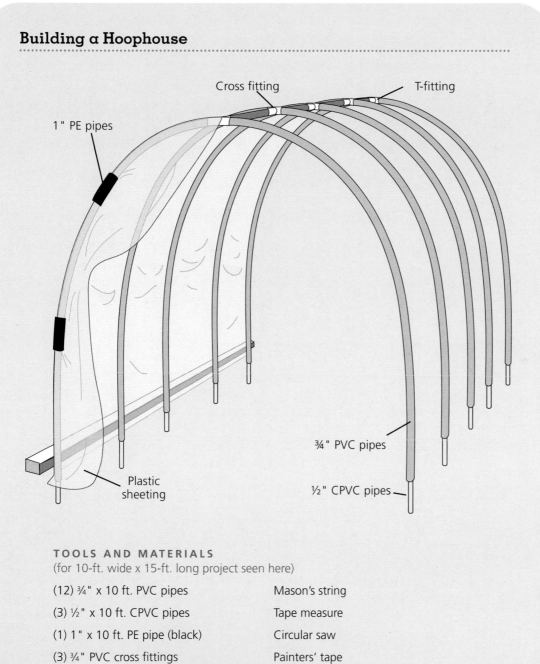

Cross fitting

T-fitting

1 " PE pipes

¾ " PVC pipes

½ " CPVC pipes

Plastic
sheeting

TOOLS AND MATERIALS
(for 10-ft. wide x 15-ft. long project seen here)

(12) ¾" x 10 ft. PVC pipes

(3) ½" x 10 ft. CPVC pipes

(1) 1" x 10 ft. PE pipe (black)

(3) ¾" PVC cross fittings

(2) ¾" PVC T-fittings

20 x 16 ft. clear or translucent
  plastic sheeting

(4) 12-ft. pressure-treated 2 x 4

Stakes

Mason's string

Tape measure

Circular saw

Painters' tape

Mallet

Maul

Stapler

2½" deck screws

Drill

How to Build a Hoophouse

1 Lay out the installation area using stakes and mason's string. Strive for square corners, but keep in mind that these are relatively forgiving structures, so you can miss by a little bit and probably won't be able to notice.

2 Cut a 30"-long stake from ½" CPVC supply tubing for each leg of each hoop frame. Measure out from the corners of the layout and attach a piece of high-visibility tape on the string at 3-ft. intervals; then drive a stake at each location. When the stake is fully driven, 10" should be above ground and 20" below.

3 Join the two legs for each frame hoop with a fitting. Use a tee fitting for the end hoop frames and a cross fitting for the intermediate hoop frames. No priming or solvent gluing is necessary. (The friction-fit should be sufficient, but it helps if you tap on the end of the fitting with a mallet to seat it.)

4 Slip the open end of one hoop-frame leg over a corner stake so the pipe is flush against the ground. Then bend the pipes so you can fit the other leg end over the stake at the opposite corner. If you experience problems with the pipes pulling out of the top fitting, simply tape the joints temporarily until the structure frame is completed.

5 Continue adding hoop frames until you reach the other end of the structure. Wait until all the hoop frames are in place before you begin installing the ridge poles. Make sure the cross fittings on the intermediate hoop frames are aligned correctly to accept the ridge poles.

6 Add the ridge-pole sections between the hoop frames. Pound on the end of each new section as you install it to seat it fully into the fitting. Install all of the poles.

continued

How to Build a Hoophouse (continued)

7 Cut four pieces of pressure-treated 2 × 4 to the length of the hoophouse (12 ft. as shown). Cut the roof cover material to size. (We used 6-mil polyethylene sheeting.) It should be several inches longer than is necessary in each direction. Tack the cover material at one end of the 2 × 4 and then continue tacking it as you work your way toward the end. Make sure the material stays taut and crease-free as you go.

8 Lay a second 2 × 4 the same length as the first over the tacked plastic so the ends and edges of the 2 × 4s are flush. Drive a 2½" deck screw through the top 2 × 4 and into the lower one every 24" or so, sandwiching the cover material between the boards. Lay the assembly next to one edge of the hoophouse and pull the free end of the material over the tops of the frames.

9 On the other side of the structure, extend the cover material all the way down so it is taut and then position another 2 × 4 underneath the fabric where it meets the ground. Staple the plastic and then sandwich it with a final 2 × 4.

10 Make clips to secure the roof cover material from a 12"-long section of hose or soft tubing. Here, 1"-dia., thin-walled PE supply tubing is slit longitudinally and then slipped over the material to clip it to the end frames. Use at least six clips per end. Do not clip at the intermediate hoop frames.

11 Option: Make doors by clipping a piece of cover material to each end. (It's best to do this before attaching the main cover.) Then cut a slit down the center of the end material. You can tie or tape the door material to the sides when you want it open and weigh down the pieces with a board or brick to keep the door shut. This solution is low-tech but effective.

Preserving Your Bounty

Preserving garden produce does not need to be an overwhelming task, but it is important to think through your strategy before you get started. To understand how to preserve food, it's important first to understand why fresh fruits and vegetables spoil and decay. There are two main culprits: First, external agents, such as bacteria and mold, break down and consume fresh food. Second, naturally occurring enzymes—the very same ones that cause fruits and veggies to ripen—are also responsible for their decay. Canning, freezing, drying, and cold storage (along with salt-curing/smoking, and making fruit preserves) are all ways to slow down or halt these processes while retaining (to varying degrees) nutrition and taste.

Each method for preserving food has its strengths and weaknesses. It's important to weigh these carefully and decide which preservation method is the best fit for your garden's needs and your lifestyle.

TIP

Drying Produce

An electric food dehydrator is a fast, effective tool for drying fruit and vegetables. Because the produce is dried quickly in a closed environment, the process is very sanitary and yields consistent, predictable results.

Canning is one of the most popular forms of food preservation. The process is reliable and can be applied to a wide variety of vegetables.

Choosing the Best Preservation Method

Produce	Canning (See page 82)	Freezing (See page 81)	Dehydration (See page 84)	Live Storage (See page 92)
Apples	✔		✔	✔
Asparagus	✔	✔		
Beans (green)	✔	✔		
Beans (lima)	✔	✔	✔	
Beets	✔			✔
Broccoli		✔	✔	
Brussel Sprouts			✔	✔
Cabbage				✔
Carrots	✔	✔		✔
Cauliflower		✔		
Celery				✔
Cherries	✔		✔	
Corn	✔	✔		
Cucumbers	✔ (with pickling)			
Onions				✔
Pears	✔		✔	✔
Peaches	✔	✔	✔	
Peas	✔	✔	✔	
Peppers (green)		✔	✔	
Peppers (hot)			✔	
Potatoes	✔			✔
Pumpkin	✔			✔
Radishes				✔
Spinach	✔	✔		
Squash (summer)	✔	✔	✔	
Squash (winter)	✔			✔
Strawberries		✔	✔	
Tomatoes	✔	✔	✔	

Canning. Canning changes the taste of foods and results in some vitamin loss, but is versatile and can be used to preserve many different kinds of foods for lengthy periods of time.

Cellaring. Live storage preserves produce with minimal effect on taste or nutritional value, but it only makes sense for a few foodstuffs. The fruits and vegetables that can be cellared for limited periods of time require a storage environment that must be carefully regulated.

Freezing and drying. Freezing and drying both retain a high percentage of vitamins and have a minimum effect on flavor, but only certain foods can be preserved with these methods and careful preparation and regulation is extremely important. Freezing can damage the cellular structure of fruits and vegetables, causing an unpleasant mushiness that makes them suitable only for dices and purees. Drying also changes the nature of fruits and vegetables; for example, drying fruits causes the caloric value to double or triple as the starches convert to sugars during the process.

○ Preservation by Freezing

Freezing is the best way to preserve delicate vegetables. It's also a quick process that is perfectly suited to smaller batches of food. In this process, foods should be blanched to stabilize nutrients and texture, cooled to preserve color, packaged in an airtight container, and frozen as quickly as possible. Frozen food, if properly packaged and contained within a temperature-consistent frozen environment, can be preserved for as long as a year. Of course, the longer you wait to eat your food, the more it will break down, which results in a loss of taste and freshness. Food can also absorb ambient flavors in the freezer environment, negatively affecting the taste.

Generally, the colder you keep your freezer, the longer your frozen food will stay tasting fresh. For best results, use a chest freezer instead of the little box above your refrigerator. Although chest freezers are an investment, they maintain colder temperatures more consistently than your refrigerator's freezer. The ideal temperature for your chest freezer is –5°F, and it should be no warmer than 0°. Even a few degrees above zero will cut the freezer life of your food in half.

TIP

Freezer Tip

Fill empty food containers, such as old milk jugs, with water and place them in the freezer around your frozen foods. With a freezer full of these homemade "ice packs," your freezer will stay colder much longer in the event of a power outage and the appliance will work at maximum efficiency, consuming less energy.

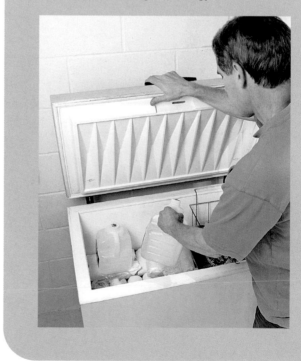

○ Preservation by Home Canning

Canning is a traditional method for preserving produce. It is not difficult to master, but it's important to pace yourself. Try not to plan more than one canning project a day to keep the work manageable and enjoyable. Also, make sure you are familiar with how to use your canning equipment safely, and that you have a reliable recipe to reference for each food you plan to can. Every fruit and vegetable has a different acidity and requires slightly different accommodations in the canning process.

To get started with canning, there are two main tools to become familiar with: a water bath canner and a pressure canner. Foods with high acidity, such as fruits (including tomatoes), can be canned in a boiling water bath. Less acidic foods, including most vegetables, and any combination of high- and low-acidity foods must be processed using a pressure canner. Water bath and pressure canners are NOT interchangeable, largely because they reach vastly different temperatures during their processes. Always make sure the canner you use is appropriate for the produce you're preserving and follow your canning recipe exactly.

Other tools you'll need include canning jars, measuring cups, a long-handled spoon, a funnel, a jar lifter, and cooking pots. Canning jars typically have two-piece metal lids: The metal band can be reused whereas the disc part of the lid cannot form an adequate seal more than once, and should be discarded after one use. Always inspect jars carefully before beginning: Check for nicks on the rim or cracks anywhere in the jar. Discard or repurpose any imperfect jars as they will not be able to form an adequate seal.

Make sure you understand how to use your home canning equipment before you get started. Take time to read through the manual that comes with your canner, and make sure you use the right type of home canner for the fruit or vegetable you're planning to preserve. A pressure canner and sealable canning jars with two-piece lids are shown here.

○ The Home Canning Process

1. **Wash and heat the jars.** Immerse jars in simmering water for at least 10 minutes or steam them for 15 minutes. Heat jar lids (just the disc part) in a small saucepan of water for at least 10 minutes. Keep lids hot, removing one at a time as needed.

2. **Pack food in the jars.** Different packing methods are used for different types of produce. In cold packing, raw food is placed in a hot jar and then hot liquid is poured over the food to fill the jar. In hot packing, foods are precooked and poured into a hot jar immediately after removing them from the heat source.

3. **Watch your headspace.** Headspace is the amount of space between the rim of the jar and the top of the food and is very important to making sure that your canning jars seal correctly. Always follow your recipe's directions—generally it's best to leave about 1" of headspace for low-acid foods, ½" for acidic foods, and ¼" for pickles, relishes, jellies, and juices.

4. **Remove air bubbles.** Insert a nonmetal spatula or chopstick and agitate the food to remove all air bubbles.

5. **Place the lid.** Clean the jar rim, then set a hot disc on the jar rim and screw on the band until you meet the initial point of resistance and no further.

6. **Heat.** Place jars on the rack in the water bath or pressure canner and process immediately. Follow the directions for your canner.

7. **Cool.** Allow the jars to cool slowly after processing—cooling too quickly can cause breakage. Typically, jars should cool along with the water they're submerged in, but follow the directions for your canner. Do not tighten the lids unless they are very loose. As the jars cool, you'll hear them "pop" when they are properly sealed. If the jar does not seal, refrigerate and eat within the next couple days.

8. **Clean and label.** After cooling and confirming the jar's seal, wash the outside of the jar and label with the content and date.

9. **Store.** Store in a cool, dark cupboard or pantry. If a jar loses its seal during storage (i.e., if the metal disc does not pop when you remove it), the food inside is not safe to eat. Dump it on the compost bin and try a different jar.

Canned Food Safety Quiz

Ask yourself the following ten questions to determine if your home-canned food is safe to eat:

1. Is the food in the jar covered with liquid and fully packed?
2. Has proper headspace been maintained?
3. Is the food free from moving air bubbles?
4. Does the jar have a tight seal?
5. Is the jar free from seepage and oozing from under the lid?
6. Has the food maintained a uniform color?
7. Is the liquid clear (not cloudy) and free of sediment?
8. Did the jar open with a clear "pop" or "hiss" and without any liquid spurts?
9. After opening, was the food free of any unusual odors?
10. Is the food and underside of the lid free of any cottonlike growths?

If you can answer "yes" to all of the questions, your food is probably safe. That said—if you have even a small suspicion that a jar of food is spoiled—dump it in the compost bin. Never, under any circumstances, taste food from a jar you suspect may have spoiled or lost its seal. Botulism spores have no odor, cannot be seen by our eyes, and can be fatal, even in small doses.

Sun drying in the open air is a traditional method for preserving fish, tomatoes, and peppers. Although it can be a very useful technique if specific environmental criteria are met (see next page), sun-drying generally is not a practical option for preserving garden produce in your backyard.

○ Preservation by Drying

There are many advantages to dehydrating produce from your garden. Most dehydration methods require very little extra energy other than that already provided by the sun. Also, dehydrated foods, if prepared correctly, retain much of their original beauty and nutritional value. And since foods lose so much of their mass during the dehydration process, they do not require much space to store through the winter and can easily be rehydrated to taste delicious months after the harvest.

Dehydration is a food preservation technique that has been used for centuries all around the world. Removing 80 to 90 percent of the moisture in food, it halts the growth of spoilage bacteria and makes long-term storage possible. Warm, dry air moving over the exposed surface of the food pieces will absorb moisture from the food and carry it away. The higher the temperature of the air, the more moisture it will absorb, and the greater the air movement, the faster the moisture will be carried away.

Temperature matters a lot in food drying—air at a temperature of 82° will carry away twice as much moisture as air at 62°. This process also concentrates natural sugars in the foods. The faster the food is dried, the higher its vitamin content will be and the less its chance of contamination by mold. Extremely high temperatures, however, will cause the outside surface or skin of the food to shrivel too quickly, trapping moisture that may cause spoilage from the inside out. Exposure to sunlight also speeds up the drying process, but can destroy some vitamins in foods.

Often, foods should be treated before drying. Blanching as you would for freezing (see page 81) is recommended for just about any vegetable (notable exceptions being onions and mushrooms). Some fruit and vegetables dry best if cut into pieces, whereas others should be left whole. Coating the produce can help preserve the bright color of skins. Many dipping mixtures may be used (consult a recipe book), but lemon juice is probably the most common.

In the following pages, we'll discuss a few different food dehydration options—both outdoor and indoor, and show you how to build drying trays and an outdoor solar dryer.

Apples are a favorite fruit for drying because they retain so much of their flavor. Look for sweet varieties like Fuji. Core them and cut them into ⅛"-thick rings or slices for drying. Peeling is optional. Dip the apples in lemon juice immediately after cutting or peeling to prevent browning.

Load food onto a drying tray and place it in a sunny, warm spot. Place the tray on wood blocks to promote air circulation from all sides. Cover the food with cheesecloth to prevent insects from reaching the food. Prop the cheesecloth above the food with blocks and toothpicks and weigh down all edges with scrap lumber.

○ Drying Produce on Trays

If you live in an area with clean air, a dry climate, and consistently sunny weather around harvest-time, you can have some success sun-drying food. The chief ingredients you'll need are time and the right weather: 85 to 100° and low to moderate humidity for several consecutive days. You'll also need a place to set your food so it receives good air circulation but is not exposed to pollution from vehicles.

- Use either stainless-steel or a nonmetallic material for your food-drying screens. Metal screen materials could be coated with chemicals that contaminate food.
- Spread your food on the trays in a single layer so the pieces do not touch one another.
- Protect your food from insects with cheesecloth—drape the cloth over wooden blocks to keep it from touching the food, and weigh down all of its edges with scrap lumber so it doesn't blow away.
- Place your trays on top of blocks at least six inches tall to promote air circulation on all sides.

Drying food outdoors will likely take at least two to three days, and perhaps longer. At dusk each day, bring the trays indoors. Cool nights can restore moisture, which not only slows down the drying process, it can also cause mold to grow. Better yet, if you have an indoor drying method—such as a food dehydrator or one of the other methods on page 90—it's a good idea to keep the drying process going at night if you can. The food will dry much faster and this lessens the chance of mold growth.

○ Solar Dryer

A solar dryer is a drying tool that makes it possible to air-dry produce even when conditions are less than ideal. This dryer is easy to make, lightweight, and is space efficient. The dryer makes a great addition to your self-sufficient home, allowing you to use your outdoor space for more than gardening. The dryer, which is made of cedar or pine, utilizes a salvaged window for a cover. But you will have to adjust the dimensions given here for the size window that you find. The key to successful solar drying is to check the dryer frequently to make sure that it stays in the sun. If the air becomes cool and damp, the food will become a haven for bacteria. In a sunny area, your produce will dry in a couple days. Add a thermometer to the inside of your dryer box, and check on the temperature frequently—it should stay between 95 and 145°F. You may choose to dry any number of different vegetables and fruits in the dryer, such as:

- Tomatoes
- Squash
- Peppers
- Bananas
- Apples

An old glass window sash gets new life as the heat–trapping cover of this solar dryer.

Building a Solar Dryer

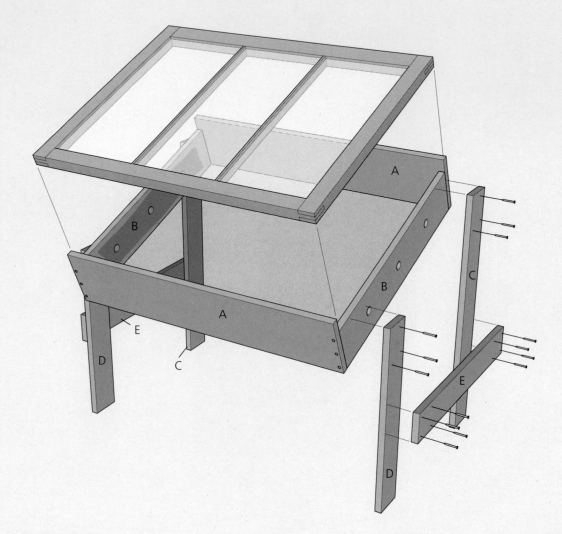

CUTTING LIST

Key	Part	No.	Dimension	Material
A	Front/back	2	¾ x 7½ x 34¾"	Cedar
B	Side	2	¾ x 5½ x 27⅛"	Cedar
C	Leg (tall)	2	¾ x 3½ x 30"	Cedar
D	Leg (short)	2	¾ x 3½ x 22"	Cedar
E	Brace	2	¾ x 3½ x 24"	Cedar

Insect Mesh—fiberglass 28⅞ x 34¾"

TOOLS & MATERIALS

1" spade bit	1¼" deck screws
Circular saw	Drill
(1) 1 x 8" x 8ft.	Staples
(1) 1 x 6" x 8ft.	Insect mesh
Eye protection	Window sash
(2) 1 x 4" x 8ft.	1½" galv. finish nails
Stapler	Brad nails

How to Build a Solar Dryer

1 Assemble the box. Attach the wider boards for the frame by driving screws through the faces of the 1 × 8" boards into the ends of the 1 × 6" boards. There will be a difference in height between these pairs of boards so that the window sash can sit flush in the recess created.

2 Install the mesh. Staple the screen to the frame. Then tack the retainer strips over the screen to the frame with 3-4 brad nails per side. Trim off the excess mesh.

3 Build the stand. Attach each 24" board to a 30" board (in the back) and a 22" board (in the front) with 1¼" deck screws. Then attach the finished posts to the frame with three 1¼" deck screws in each post.

4 Drill three 1" holes for ventilation in each 1 × 6" board equally spaced along the length of the board, leaving 5" of room on each end for the posts. Staple leftover insect mesh behind the ventilation holes on the inside of the frame.

5 Finish the project by sliding the window sash into place.

○ Drying Produce Indoors

Drying vegetables indoors allows you to carefully control the drying conditions and offers more protection from insects and changes in weather. An electric food dehydrator appliance is the simplest choice for indoor drying. If you don't have a dehydrator, the next best option is in or around your oven, although any hot, dry area will do—possibly even your attic or the area around a heater or cookstove.

If you plan to dry produce in your oven, keep in mind that the process typically takes eight to twelve hours. Preheat your oven and check that it can maintain a temperature of 130 to 145° for at least an hour—some ovens have a difficult time holding low temperatures like this, and going over 150° can be disastrous for drying produce. Wash and prepare the food, then spread food in single layers on baking sheets, making sure the pieces do not touch. Place the sheets directly on the oven racks, leaving at least 4" above and below for air circulation. Also, make sure to leave the oven door slightly ajar to allow moisture to escape. Rearrange the trays and shift food from time to time to ensure even drying.

You may also dry food on your oven's range by creating a chafing dish. To create a chafing dish on your range, you'll need two baking trays: The first must be large enough to cover all burners and hold a 3"-deep reservoir of water. The second tray should fit on top of the first. Fill the bottom tray with water and set all burners to low heat. Throughout the process, refill the reservoir periodically to make sure food doesn't burn, and move/turn food as necessary to ensure even drying. Place a fan nearby to keep the air moving around the room, which will help carry moisture away from the food more quickly.

When drying produce in the oven, leave the door slightly ajar to allow moisture to escape, and carefully monitor temperature to ensure the oven doesn't heat to over 150°.

An electric produce dehydrator can dry large quantities of fruits or vegetables in a sanitary environment. The stackable trays allow you to match the appliance's drying capacity to your needs each time you use it.

How Long Does Dehydration Take?

Drying times vary considerably—from a few hours to many days, depending on the climate, humidity, drying method, and the moisture content of the food you're dehydrating. Generally, fruit is done drying if it appears leathery and tough and no moisture can be squeezed from it. Vegetables should be so brittle and crisp that they rattle on the tray. To check for completed dehydration, you can also check the food's weight before and after the process. If the food has lost half its weight, it is two-thirds dry, so you should continue to dry for half the time you've already dried.

To double-check that your food is dry, place it in a wide-rimmed, open-topped bowl covered with cheesecloth fastened with a rubber band. Place the bowl in a dry place, and keep the food in the bowl for about a week. Stir it a couple times a day—if any moisture or condensation appears, you should continue to dehydrate.

Pasteurization and Storage

Regardless of the drying method used, food should be pasteurized before storage to ensure that there are no insect eggs or spoilage microorganisms present. To pasteurize, preheat the oven to 175°. Spread dried food 1" deep on trays and bake in the oven for 10 to 15 minutes. Dried food is best stored in clean glass jars or plastic bags in a cool, dry place. Never store dried food in metal containers and carefully monitor the humidity of the storage environment. Containers should have tight-fitting lids and should be stored in a dark, dry place with an air temperature below 60°.

> **TIP**
>
> **Enjoying Your Dehydrated Food**
>
> Many foods are delicious and ready to eat in their dried forms—especially tomatoes and berries. But dried food can also be rehydrated before eating. To rehydrate food, pour boiling water over it in a ratio of 1½ cups of water to 1 cup of dried food, then let the food soak until all the water has been absorbed. You may also steam fruit or vegetables until rehydrated. Rehydrated vegetables should be cooked before eating, whereas rehydrated fruits are acceptable to eat without cooking after rehydration.

Use your oven to heat fruits and vegetables to a high enough temperature to kill bacteria and related contaminants. About 15 minutes at 175°F will suffice for most produce, provided it is not in layers over 1″ deep. Oven-drying takes about a half day at 140° or so.

Setting Up a Root Cellar

Cool storage areas such as cellars can be outfitted to keep produce fresh for the table throughout the long winter months. A wide variety of foods will stay fresh and delicious if stored in the right conditions—a space that is damp and cold, but not freezing. Typically, 32 to 40 degrees Fahrenheit is ideal for a root cellar environment. This type of food storage is entirely dependent on thermal mass and the natural cooling of outdoor air during the winter, and this isn't vulnerable to power outages. Traditionally, root cellars are an underground space built under or near the home, insulated by the ground and vented so cold air can flow in and warm air out in the fall. In the winter, the vents are then closed and the cellar maintains a cold— but not freezing—temperature, thanks to the earth's insulation.

Of course a walk-in root cellar built like this is the most reliable solution, but you can still practice cold storage without an external walk-in root cellar. The best systems are adapted to each home and climate, and can be as simple as a deep hole in the yard that is carefully covered, to a homemade basement cold room, like the one described on page 95.

A root cellar doesn't actually need to be underground, although they often are. Any cool, dark area will do.

How to Store Produce in a Root Cellar

Vegetable	Will Store For...	Special Instructions
Apples	5 to 8 months	Apples give off a gas that causes root vegetables to sprout or spoil, so store them in separate spaces. Apples also like to be moist—and store well in a barrel lined with paper or sawdust.
Cabbage and Cauliflower	Cabbage—3 to 4 months Cauliflower—1 month Chinese Cabbage—2 months	Store only sound, solid heads. Place the heads in plastic bags that have a few holes to let excess moisture escape. Remove roots and outer leaves.
Carrots and Parsnips	4 to 6 months	Snip off the leaves just above the crown. Store in covered containers filled with moist sand or moss.
Celery	2 to 3 months	Harvest just before heavy frost. Leave the roots and soil attached and set in moist sand in a shallow container on the cellar floor. The sand should be only deep enough to cover the roots and must be kept slightly moist. Cover or store in the dark.
Hot Peppers	6 months	Air dry and store in a cool, well-ventilated room.
Pears	3 months	Pack in loose paper in crates or barrels.
Potatoes and other Root Vegetables	Beets—3 months Potatoes—5 to 8 months Turnips—4 to 5 months	Cut off the tops about ½" above the crown. Store bedded in vented plastic bags or covered crates filled with damp sphagnum moss or sand. Keep out of light. Note that potatoes like to be stored a little warmer—around 40°.
Pumpkins and Squash	Pumpkins—3 months Squash—6 months	Leave a part of the stem on each pumpkin or squash. Pumpkins and squash thrive in a slightly warmer space—between 55 and 60°. Keep pumpkins and squash dry—a humid space will cause them to deteriorate.
Onions and Garlic	Onions—8 months Garlic—7 months	Pull when tops fall over and begin to dry. When tops are completely dry, cut them off 1" from the bulbs. Cure for another week or two before placing in storage. Onions and garlic are best kept dry and stored in mesh bags or crates.

How to Set Up a Basement Root Cellar

Modern basements are typically too warm for long-term winter storage, but you can create an indoor version of a root cellar by walling off and insulating a basement corner and adding vents to the outside to let you regulate the flow of cold outside air into the insulated room. Your goal is to create a small room that is well insulated and will remain near freezing throughout the winter months. Cellar rooms are typically quite humid, so be sure to choose insulation materials that will hold up well in a moist environment.

First, choose a location for your cellar that is as far as possible from your furnace, and near a basement window, if possible. The window is a great place to install a vent—simply remove the window glass, replace it with insulated plywood, and run the vent through a hole in the wood. (You could also run a vent through a basement wall—as you would for a clothes dryer.) Choose a northeast or northwest corner location if you can. The more masonry surface in your root cellar room, the better—masonry walls provide thermal insulation to help create the ideal temperature inside. If a northeast or northwest corner won't work for your basement, choose the corner with the highest outdoor soil height.

Store only mature, high-quality vegetables in a root cellar: small, cut, bruised, or broken vegetables will not store well and should be eaten right away. Check on your stored foods frequently to see how they're doing—if the vegetables begin to grow, the cellar is too warm. If they freeze, the cellar is too cold. If the skin starts to look dry or shriveled, the space is too dry. Remove decaying vegetables immediately to prevent rot from spreading to the rest of your food.

To Store Carrots: Cut off greens and wrap them in small groups of newspaper. Bury paper packages in dry sand.

Building a Root Cellar

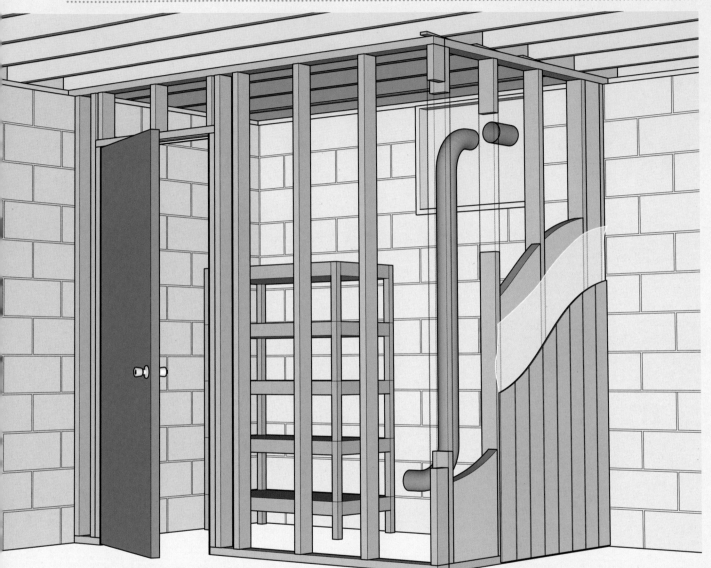

TOOLS & MATERIALS

Chalk	Drill	Stapler	Masking tape
Eye protection	Level	Stick up light	4d finish nails
Ear protection	Deck screws	Fiberglass butt insulation	Glue
Construction adhesive	Circulating saw	Paneling or drywall	Wood screws
Concrete nails	Insect mesh	Steel garage service door	Framing square
Powder-actuated nail gun	Sheet plastic vapor barrier	Weather stripping	Sander
	Foam insulation		

How to Add a Root Cellar to a Basement

1 Outline the root cellar wall locations on your basement floor with chalk or a chalkline. Don't get too skimpy—the foot-print should be at least 4 × 6 ft. to make the project worthwhile.

2 Build 2 × 4 stud walls with a framed rough opening for a door. Anchor the sole plates for the walls (use pressure-treated lumber) to the floor with construction adhesive and concrete nails driven into predrilled holes (or use a powder-actuated nail gun).

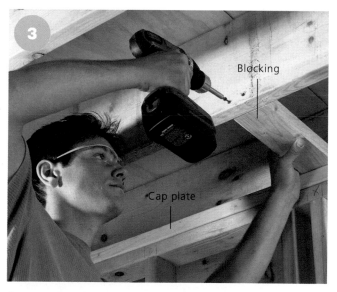

Blocking

Cap plate

3 Use a level to adjust the walls until they are plumb and then secure the cap plates of the framed walls to the joists above with deck screws. If the cap plate on the wall that's parallel to the joists does not align with a joist, you'll need to install wood blocking between the joists to have a nailing surface for the cap plate.

4 Insulate the interior walls to keep the ambient basement heat out of the root cellar. Rigid foam insulation is a great choice for root cellar walls, since it is more resistant to mold and deterioration from moisture than fiberglass batts.

continued

How to Add a Root Cellar to a Basement (continued)

5 Staple a sheet-plastic vapor barrier to the basement side of the walls where condensation is likely to form.

6 Also insulate the ceiling. Line the joist cavities above the root cellar with sheet plastic before you install the insulation to create a vapor barrier there (the vapor barrier always goes on the warm side of the insulation). Use faced fiberglass batt insulation, or use unfaced fiberglass and install a ceiling covering such as paneling.

7 Install a wall covering, such as paneling or drywall, over the vapor barrier on the basement side (required for fire resistance). You may cover the wall on the root-cellar side if you wish—there is little point in doing it for aesthetic reasons, but the wallcovering will protect the insulation from damage.

8 Hang the door. A steel garage service door with a foam core is durable and well insulated. Be sure to install weatherstripping around the door to create a seal that minimizes heat transfer.

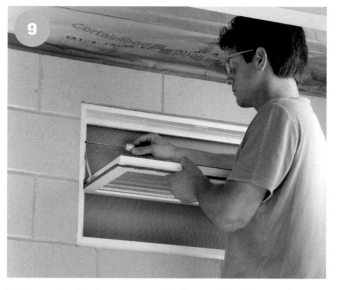

9 Remove the basement window sash, if your cellar area has a window. (If not, install a vent in the rim joist—find information on installing a dryer vent for guidance.) Keep the window stop molding in the jambs intact if you can.

10 Make a ventilation insert panel to replace the window. The panel should have an outflow vent with a manually operated damper so you can regulate the temperature by letting warmer air escape. It should also have an intake vent with ductwork that helps direct cold air down to floor level. On the exterior side, cover the vent openings with insect mesh to prevent rodents and insects from gaining access to your cellar.

11 Install the ventilation panel insert in the window frame by nailing or screwing it up against the stop molding. Caulk around the edge to prevent insects from getting in. Paint or cover the outside of the panel to weatherproof it.

12 Provide lighting. If you do not want to install a new, hardwired light and switch (this should be done before walls are covered if you do it), install a stick-up light that operates on battery power. A model with LED bulbs will run for months of intermittent use without a battery change. Add racks and storage features (see next page).

How to Build a Root Cellar Shelf

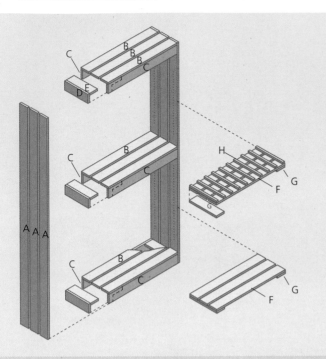

CUTTING MATERIALS

Key	Part	Dimension
A	(6) Side slat	¾ × 3½ × 84" pine
B	(9) Fixed-shelf slat	¾ × 3½ × 30½" pine
C	(6) Fixed-shelf face	¾ × 3½ × 30½" pine
D	(6) Fixed-shelf end	¾ × 3½ × 10½" pine
E	(6) Fixed-shelf stretcher	¾ × 3½ × 10½" pine
F	(6) Adjustable shelf slat	¾ × 3½ × 30⅜" pine
G	(4) Adjustable shelf stretcher	¾ × 3½ × 12" pine
H	(10) Bottle-shelf cleat	¾ × ¾ × 12" pine

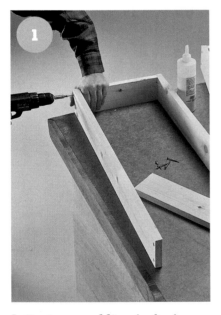

1 Begin assembling the fixed shelves by cutting the ends and faces to size, and then joining them with glue and counterbored screws. Check with a framing square to make sure the frames you're assembling are square.

2 Add the stretchers to the tops of the fixed shelf frames. In addition to strengthening the fixed shelf units, the stretchers provide nailing or screwing surfaces for attaching the shelf slats.

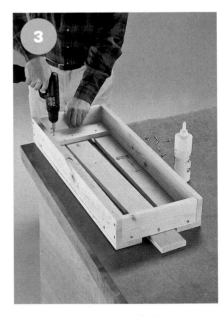

3 Cut the fixed-shelf slats to length, sand them, and attach them to the fixed shelf frames by driving 1¼" screws up through counterbored pilot holes in the stretchers and into the bottom of the slats. Keep your spacing even and make sure the slats do not overhang the frame ends.

4 Cut the side slats to length, sand them, and attach them to the outside of the fixed shelf units with glue and counterbored wood screws. Make sure the spacing (¾" between slats) is correct and that all joints are square.

5 Drill adjustable shelf peg holes in the side slats. To ensure good results, make a drilling template from a piece of perforated hardboard. Use a drill bit the same diameter as your shelf pins, and drill the holes ½" deep. Use masking tape as a drilling depth gauge.

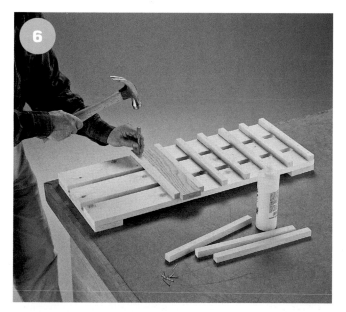

6 Build an adjustable shelf to support a bottle (wine, for instance) rack, using a 2½" wide spacer to set the distances separating the shelf cleats. Attach the cleats to the shelf with glue and 4d finish nails. Make the other adjustable shelf.

7 Insert shelf pins and install the adjustable shelves. Fill screw-hole counterbores with wood plugs, trim flush, and sand. Finish the shelf as desired. Because it is for indoor use, you may leave it unfinished for a rustic look if you prefer.

Raising Animals

Raising small farm animals can be a challenge and it is a serious responsibility, but once you've taken the plunge the rewards can be so great that it is very difficult to go back. You'll find a number of reasons why chickens and other small animals can be a great addition to the self-sufficient home: In addition to the companionship and fun they provide, they can be a great source of wool, milk, meat, and eggs (depending on species of course).

If your animal experience is limited to walking your dog and emptying the cat box, it's a good idea for you to start small in your livestock adventure. Chickens are an excellent indoctrination—they require little space, are easy to care for, and provide the reward of fresh eggs and/or lean, free range meat. As you consider which animals you'd like to purchase, consider how different species will fit your land, temperament, experience, and time allowance. If you're a beginner, wait until you grow more confident before adopting notoriously flighty sheep, or a conniving goat that will try to outsmart you.

Also, it's important to select animals that will be comfortable on your property. How hot or cold is the region where you live? While you can make accommodations by choosing the right shelter for your animal, some extreme climates simply are not suitable for every animal. Before you purchase livestock, contact local veterinarians and find out whether they will treat the species you plan to buy. If you cannot find a vet in your area who will treat the llama you're planning to purchase, find out how far you'll have to drive

Chickens are probably the most popular farm animal when it comes to fitting in to a city lifestyle (see Building a Chicken Ark, page 115). In recent years, many larger cities have relaxed their restrictions on keeping animals, so if you've been turned down in the past it might be worth checking again.

to reach someone who will, and weigh this into your decision. Also, think through the logistics of how you will transport your animal and the time it will take to reach the vet.

Lastly, check with your municipality to find out what the limitations are when it comes to owning livestock. If you live in the city, you may need to request permission from your neighbors to house animals, and some species may not be allowed at all. There may also be setback requirements that apply to animal housing—take these into consideration when planning out the site for your animals' home.

Match Your Shelter to Your Animal

Pigs

Chickens

Horses

Sheep

Goats

Rabbits

Every species has different needs regarding the type of shelter they require to grow up healthfully. Research the specific needs of your animal before you build a new shelter or convert an existing one.

○ Animal Infrastructure

Before you introduce animals to your backyard, prepare your property for their arrival. Think of it as building a nest—consider where the animals will sleep, what they will eat, and where they will roam and play. Build fencing and shelter, provide a water source and feed area, and find a dependable veterinarian who can administer immunizations. You'll also need to determine whether your property is zoned for the type of animals you want to raise, what limits apply in terms of animal shelter setbacks, grazing requirements, and whether or not you'll need to apply for licenses, permits, and community permission.

A barn is not necessary for every species, though most animals require some type of shelter for protection from the elements and, perhaps, for sleeping. The type of roof you put over animals' heads depends largely on where you live. In the chilly north, animals will require a more sturdy, draft-resistant abode than in the hot and dry southwest. Build your shelter to suit your climate—in cold climates, your shelter should be designed to keep animals warm, and in warm climates, designed to keep animals cool. Tailor your shelter to meet your animals' needs. For example, pigs require separate space for eating and sleeping, whereas sheep and goats just need a dry shelter to protect them from the elements.

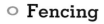

Fencing

The species of animals you keep will determine the kind of fencing you should build to protect them. Goats are especially tricky and will gnaw and break through fencing. Your best bet for goats is a woven-wire fence with posts of steel or wood, with added protection from two strands of barbed wire, one at the top and one at the bottom of the fence. Pigs like to outsmart fencing systems, hence the phrase "hog-tight fence." Build a fence of woven wire or permanent wood at least three feet tall.

Some species really do not care to try to get out, but you do need a fence to protect them from predators. A fence tall enough to keep out predators in your area—typically five feet or so—will work for these animals.

A good, strong fence is the best insurance you can obtain for goats, hogs, and other animals with a strong sense of wanderlust.

Pigs love attention and are infinitely curious. Be sure to build a strong fence around your pigpen to keep your pigs contained.

○ Pigs

Pigs are personable and intelligent. They also offer a well-rounded learning experience for new animal owners: lessons on the importance of feed mix, daily pigpen cleaning to prevent disease (and smell!), and good old-fashioned recycling. Their composted byproduct is rich fertilizer for your garden.

Pigs don't require a great deal of land, but they do need a dry, draft-free shelter to protect them from the elements. Be sure to prepare this space before bringing home your new pets. You can dedicate a portion of an existing building, such as a barn or shelter, or construct a simple outbuilding. Ideally, the floor should be concrete and sloped for optimal drainage during daily hose-outs. A dirt floor is also fine as long as you replace hay bedding daily.

Pigs also require a separate sleeping and feeding area. A five foot by five foot square sleeping area will accommodate two pigs. The feed area should be twice this size and contain the feed trough, a watering system, and a hose connection. This serves the double purpose of instant water refills for thirsty pigs and accessibility to your number one pigpen-cleaning tool.

Contain your pigs with a secure fence of woven wire or permanent board (see page 108). The fence should be about three feet tall. Pigs are immensely social animals and love the spotlight, so be sure to spend time with them to help them grow healthy and happy.

Goats are high-spirited, lovable, and mischievous animals that love to play. Watch out, though—your goats will try to outsmart you (or your fence!). Goats are a great source of milk, wool, and meat.

○ Goats

Goats are mischievous class clowns with boundless energy and a lovable nature. They are a great source of both milk and meat, and do not require a vast amount of resources, food, or shelter. They are ruminants that enjoy munching twigs and leafy brush—but if you will be raising goats for their milk, feed them with a forage of hay and grain to preserve their milk's taste. Some goat breeds are also a great source of fibers for fabrics, such as mohair and angora. You'll want to watch these breeds' diets carefully, as their coat will be affected by their diet. Feed them only quality pasture or hay, along with plenty of fresh, clean water.

There's no need to build a fancy house for goats, as they fare well in pretty much any dry, draft-free quarters. Goats are prone to respiratory problems triggered by a moist environment, so avoid heating that can result in condensation. House goats in a three-sided barn, shed, or a shared barn with other animals. It's a good idea to invest your savings on shelter in quality fencing, however. Woven-wire pasture fencing is ideal, and additional strands of barbed or electrical wire will discourage curious goats from escaping.

Sheep

Sheep are affectionate animals raised most often for their high-quality wool that can be spun into yarn and made into warm textiles. Choose a breed of sheep with a wool density that correlates with the weather where you live—in the north, choose sheep with extra "lining" in their coats; in temperate or arid climates, sheep with fine wool and hair prosper.

When purchasing sheep, look for healthy feet. From the front view, legs and hooves should align, as opposed to being knock-kneed, splayfooted, or pigeon-toed. Check the animal's bite, and be sure there are no udder lumps or skin lesions. Sheep do need to be shorn every spring before the weather heats up, so take good care of your sheep's wool and sell or spin it after it is collected. To care for your sheep (and their wool), make sure they have good nutrition, well-managed pastures, and vaccinations. Sheep need a sturdy fence and some type of shelter, though existing buildings on your land will suit them just fine. They are easy targets for predators, such as coyotes, so make certain your fence is secure.

Alpacas

Alpacas are smaller cousins to llamas and camels and are an approachable, friendly species, which makes them appealing to landowners who want to begin caring for animals. They won't challenge your fencing or trample your pasture. They also require little feed—about a third less than a sheep. Alpacas grow thick coats that are five times warmer than wool and far more durable. Yarn spinners covet alpaca fiber, homeowners admire these loving pets, and investors appreciate the potential returns these valuable creatures promise.

Fencing you'll build for alpacas is designed more to keep predators out than to keep alpacas in. These animals are not ambitious escape artists—not nearly as tricky as goats. But predators can represent a threat to sensitive alpacas, so it's a good idea to install strong perimeter fencing that is at least five feet tall. Separate females and males with fencing. Females and their newborns must have separate quarters from the rest of the pack, but do not completely isolate them from the group. A three-sided shelter is adequate for alpacas, which are accustomed to rugged, cold climates. Heat is more of a concern for these animals, and their insulating fiber coats are no help in keeping them cool in summer. A misting system or fans in the alpaca shelter will prevent them from overheating.

Sheep travel in close-knit packs, are spooked easily, and are an easy target for predators, so make sure your sheep are protected by a secure fence.

Lock eyes with a quizzical alpaca and you'll feel like you are being probed for information. Alpacas are gentle animals that are easy to care for and produce soft, extremely warm coats that can be shorn and sold to textile makers.

Vinyl fencing is durable and virtually maintenance free. However, damaged pieces are expensive to replace and materials can cost up to twice as much as a traditional wood fence. For these reasons, most landowners use vinyl to enclose smaller areas.

○ Fences

Fencing plays a critical role in controlling animals, keeping out predators, sectioning off pastures, drawing property lines, and adding aesthetic appeal to properties. Your fencing needs will vary depending on the size of your lot and what type of animals call your land home (pigs, chickens, horses). Hobby farms will require functional fences, but if you live on a country estate, the reasons for your fence may be purely aesthetic. There are materials and designs that accommodate both goals.

Fence Materials

Progress in fencing is evident in the type of materials available, synthetics like PVC, and the improved life expectancy of good old standards like wood and wire, which can be treated with a vinyl coating. High-tensile wire fencing can last up to 50 years. But the more traditional types, such as split-rail, Virginia rail, and post-and-rail, will always have their place.

Before choosing fencing material, ask yourself the following: How large is the area to be fenced? What is the purpose of your fence? Will you install it yourself or hire a professional? How much are you willing to spend?

Utilitarian by design, yet pleasing to the eye, the post and board fence evokes the uncomplicated beauty and peacefulness of rolling countryside. The same effect holds true in suburban settings.

○ Post & Board Fences

Post and board fences include an endless variety of simple designs in which widely spaced square or round posts support several horizontal boards. This type of fence has been around since the early 1700s, when it began to be praised for its efficient use of lumber and land and its refined appearance. The post and board is still a great design today. Even in a contemporary suburban setting, a classic, white three- or four-board fence evokes the stately elegance of a horse farm or the welcoming, down-home feel of a farmhouse fence bordering a country lane.

Another desirable quality of post and board fencing is its ease in conforming to slopes and rolling ground. In fact, it often looks best when the fence rises and dips with ground contours. Of course, you can also build the fence so it's level across the top by trimming the posts along a level line. Traditional agricultural versions of post and board fences typically include three to five boards spaced evenly apart or as needed to contain livestock. If you like the look of widely spaced boards but need a more complete barrier for pets, cover the back side of the fence with galvanized wire fencing, which is relatively unnoticeable behind the bold lines of the fence boards. You can also use the basic post and board structure to create any number of custom designs. The fence styles shown in the following pages are just a sampling of what you can build using the basic construction technique for post and board fences.

A low post and board fence, like traditional picket fencing, is both decorative and functional, creating a modest enclosure without blocking views. The same basic fence made taller and with tighter board spacing becomes an attractive privacy screen or security fence.

How to Build a Post & Board Fence

1 Set the posts in concrete, following the desired spacing. Laying out the posts at 96" on center allows for efficient use of lumber. For smaller boards, such as 1 × 4s and smaller, set posts closer together for better rigidity.

2 Trim and shape the posts with a circular saw. For a contoured fence, measure up from the ground and mark the post height according to your plan (post height shown here is 36"). For a level fence, mark the post heights with a level string. If desired, cut a 45° chamfer on the post tops using a speed square to ensure straight cuts. Prime and paint (or stain and seal) the posts.

3 Mark the board locations by measuring down from the top of each post and making a mark representing the top edge of each board. Use a speed square to draw a line across the front faces of the posts at each height mark. Mark the post centers on alternate posts using a combination square or speed square and pencil. For strength, it's best to stagger the boards so that butted end joints occur at every other post. The centerlines represent the location of each butted joint.

4 Install 1 × 6 boards. Measure and mark each board for length, and then cut it to size. Clamp the board to the posts, following the height and center marks. Drill pilot holes and fasten each board end with three 2½" deck screws or 8d galvanized box nails. Use three fasteners where long boards pass over posts as well.

Virginia Rail Fence

The Virginia rail fence—also called a worm, snake, or zigzag fence—was actually considered the national fence by the U.S. Department of Agriculture prior to the advent of wire fences in the late 1800s. All states with farmland cleared from forests had them in abundance.

The simplest fences were built with an extreme zigzag and didn't require posts. To save on lumber and land, farmers began straightening the fences and burying pairs of posts at the rail junctures.

A variation in design that emerged with entirely straight lines is called a Kentucky rail fence.

Feel free to accommodate the overlapping rail fence we build here to suit your tastes and needs. Increase the zigzag to climb rolling ground, decrease it to stretch the fence out. All lapped rail fences should be made from rot-resistant wood like cedar, locust, or cyprus. For the most authentic-looking fence, try to find split rather than sawn logs. For longevity, raise the bottom rail off the ground with stones. Posts may eventually rot below ground, but the inherently stable zigzag form should keep the fence standing until you can replace them.

TOOLS & MATERIALS

Tools & materials for laying out the fence line

Tools & materials for setting posts

Chainsaw or reciprocating saw

Long-handled maul

Bolt cutters

Hatchet

Large screwdriver

Pliers

Clothesline rope

Work gloves

9-gauge galvanized wire

The Virginia Rail Fence exhibits a very familiar style to anyone who has spent much time in countryside that was cleared and farmed in the 18th and 19th centuries. Since nails were scarce, these zigzagging post-and-rail fences were popular because they are held together with only wire or rope.

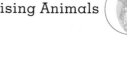

How to Build a Virginia Rail Fence

1 Create layout lines in the fence installation area for each section. Mark post locations and a main fence line with additional layout lines parallel to the fence line. The total distance between the outer lines (here, 24") equals the amount of switchback on each rail section. Dig your post holes and install your posts.

2 Bind your post pairs together at the top and place spacers on the ground for the bottom rail. Insert the bottom rail between the posts, resting on the spacers.

3 Install split fence rails in alternating courses at each post pair, keeping the overhangs even.

4 Bind the tops of the posts together permanently with 9-gauge galvanized wire to hold the rails in position. Tighten the wire by twisting with a screwdriver blade as if you were tightening a tourniquet.

Building a Chicken Ark

Chickens adapt more easily to life on a small urban homestead than other farm animals. Consequently, raising urban chickens has grown in popularity in recent years. In fact, many municipalities have relaxed their restrictions and requirements when it comes to tending a small number of hens. It's worth noting that the same latitude has not been given to roosters—typically, you must file a document with the consent of all your neighbors before the city will let you keep a loud winged alarm clock in your yard.

Chickens can live comfortably in many different types of environments, from small urban backyards to roomy farms and ranches. They have a lot to offer the self-sufficient homeowner: high-quality meat, farm-fresh eggs, new chicks, and even nitrogen-rich garden fertilizer. Chickens do require a safe place to live, especially during the night. Usually, this takes the form of a chicken coop.

A chicken coop that can be easily moved around your yard or garden offers the added benefit of distributing natural fertilizer while the chickens feast on bugs and weeds in your yard. Some gardeners even design mobile coops to cap their raised beds so the birds can be moved around to fertilize the soil and prepare it for planting in the spring. The portable coop that is built on the following pages contains both a roost with laying nests and a protected scratching area. It is large enough to accommodate four to six full

Build your chickens a safe and comfortable home that can easily be moved around your yard or garden. This type of portable coop, known as a chicken ark or a chicken tractor, should keep your birds safe from the elements and from predators.

Approvals

The first step to starting your own chicken coop is to get permission from your local municipality. Many cities and towns allow homeowners to keep hens, but no roosters. Typically, there is also a limit on the number of hens you can keep, and the distance your coop must be located from your neighbors' windows. Check the regulations in your municipality as you develop your chicken ranching plan. It's also important to talk with your neighbors to seek out their consent, even if their written permission is not required.

size hens, is attractive enough to find a home in any urban, suburban, or estate yard, and is complete with all the essential components of a coop: space for roosting, nesting boxes for laying eggs, and easy access for the bird owner to refill food and water, clean the coop and replace bedding, and to collect eggs.

NOTE: This chicken ark is made from untreated pine, so its direct exposure to the elements should be limited. Although the preserving chemicals in modern treated lumber are not considered toxic, they should not be ingested directly—and chickens tend to peck at and eat their habitats. Even woods with natural rot resistance, such as cedar, often contain chemical compounds that can cause irritation if ingested.

○ Getting Started

If you plan to raise chickens for their eggs, it's best to purchase pullets (chickens less than a year old) that have already been vaccinated and have just begun laying eggs. Pullets do not require a special brood environment, like chicks, but you should carefully monitor their light exposure and heat when they're young. Keep your pullets in the coop for a week or so to help them get accustomed to their new home.

When they are old enough, allow your hens out of the coop during the day to peck and wander around a larger enclosed area, such as a small yard surrounded by a fence. Hens will not wander far. They love to dine on the bugs and weeds in your yard, and will produce a greater yield of healthier eggs if allowed to move around freely. At night, make sure all your hens are safely locked in to the coop to sleep.

○ Collecting Eggs

Collecting eggs from a brooding hen requires a careful hand and sound timing. Expect a good pecking if you reach into the nest while mother is awake. The best time to gently remove eggs from the nest is in the morning or during the night, when hens roost. This is also the best time to pick up a hen and move her, because she won't argue while she's sleeping. Eggs may be brown, white, or sometimes even light blue or speckled—depending on the breed of your chicken. No matter the appearance, what's inside will taste the same.

Gather eggs twice a day, and even more frequently during temperature extremes when eggs are vulnerable. The longer they sit in the nest, the more likely eggs are to suffer shell damage. After gathering, pat the eggs clean with a dry cloth. If they are noticeably dirty, wash them with warm water. Place clean, dry eggs in a carton and refrigerate.

Chickens are outdoor birds and prefer to roam within limits. They are natural pest-controllers and will stay healthiest if allowed to move about for a portion of every day.

Chicken Breeds

So, why do you want chickens?

Perhaps you dream of eggs with thick, sturdy sunshine yolks that are unbeatable for baking (and perhaps for selling at a farmers' market stand). Maybe you want to dress the dinner table with a fresh bird. Not sure? If you want both eggs and meat, you're safe with a dual-purpose breed such as the barred Plymouth Rock.

Next, consider the size flock you will need to fulfill your goals. This depends on land availability and how much produce you wish to gain. In other words, if volume of eggs or meat matters, then you increase your "production line." If your reason for raising chickens is to enjoy the company of a low-maintenance feathered pet—the meat and eggs are just a bonus—then a flock of three or four hens and possibly a rooster will get you started.

Layers

While all chickens produce eggs, laying breeds are more efficient at the job than other breeds; in short, layers lay more eggs. You can expect about 250 eggs per year or more if your layer is more ambitious than most. Laying hens tend to be high-strung, however, and while they lay many eggs, they show little interest in raising chicks. You may

reconsider laying breeds if you want your hens to raise the next generation. Layers simply aren't interested—but they'll keep seconds coming to the breakfast table.

Meat Breeds

These chickens are classified based on size when butchered. Game hens weigh 1 to 3 pounds (.5 to 1.4 kg), broilers (also called fryers) range from 4 to 5 pounds (1.8 to 2.3 kg), and roasters are usually 7 pounds (3.2 kg) or slightly more. You'll find cross-breeds ideal for the backyard, including broiler-roaster hybrids like the Cornish hen or the New Hampshire.

Dual-Purpose Breeds

Larger than layers but more productive (in the egg department) than meat breeds, dual-purpose breeds are the happy medium. Hens will sit on eggs until they hatch, so you can raise the next generation. There are many chickens that fall into this variety, and their temperaments vary. Many dual-purpose breeds are also heritage breeds, meaning they are no longer bred in mass for industry. They like to forage for worms and bugs, are known for disease resistance, and, essentially, are the endangered species of the chicken world.

Chickens raised for meat usually are purchased from a hatchery or a feed store when just a day or two old. Raising them to broiler weight (4 to 5 pounds) takes six to eight weeks. During this time they will consume around 15 pounds of feed.

Ornamental chickens often make good pets. They enjoy human companionship. And they are a fun and visual addition to the yard!

Chickens do well in cold weather as long as they have a sheltered, insulated roosting area and their water supply is not allowed to freeze.

Building a Chicken Ark

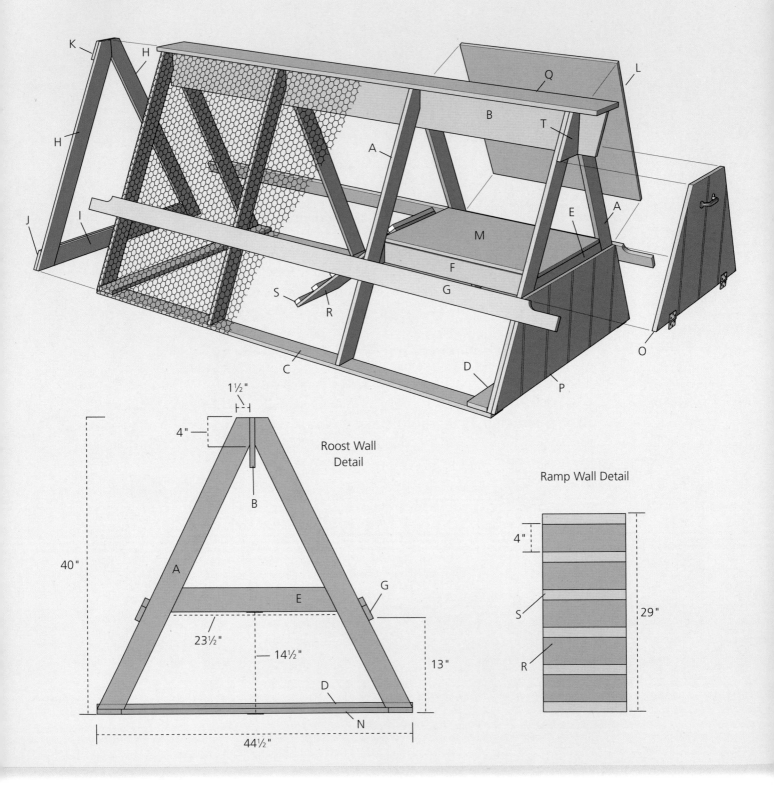

Roost Wall
Detail

1½"

4"

B

A

E

40"

23½"

14½"

13"

D

N

44½"

Ramp Wall Detail

4"

S

R

29"

CUTTING LIST

Key	Part	Dimension	Pcs.	Material
A	Rafters	¾ x 3½ x 46"	8	1 x 4 pine
B	Ridge pole	¾ x 7¼ x 86"	1	1 x 8 pine
C	Base plate	¾ x 3½ x 81"	2	1 x 4 pine
D	Spreader	¾ x 3½ x 44½"	2	1 x 4 pine
E	Roost beam	¾ x 3½ x 23½"	2	1 x 4 pine
F	Roost joist	¾ x 3½ x 26"	2	1 x 4 pine
G	Handle	¾ x 3½ x 96"	2	1 x 4 pine
H	Door stile	¾ x 3½ x 47¼"	2	1 x 4 pine
I	Door rail	¾ x 3½ x 36¾"	1	1 x 4 pine
J	Door bottom brace	¾ x 3½ x 44½"	1	1 x 4 pine
K	Door gusset	¾ x 7¼ x 8⅛"	1	1 x 8 pine
L	Roost side	½ x 27¾ x 29"	2	Siding panel
M	Roost floor	½ x 20 x 27½"	1	Siding panel
N	Base filler	¾ x 3½ x 36¾"	1	1 x 4 pine
O	Roost door	½ x 19½ x 29½"	1	Siding panel
P	End wall	½ x 44⅝ x 16⅛"	1	Siding panel
Q	Ridge board	¾ x 3½ x 88"	1	1 x 4 pine
R	Ramp	½ x 12 x 29"	1	Siding panel
S	Ramp battens	¾ x 1½ x 12"	6	1 x 2 pine
T	Roost Door Filler	½ x 1½ x 4"	2	Sliding

TOOLS & MATERIALS

Circular saw

Jigsaw

Speed square

Tape measure

Power miter saw

Drill

Galvanized wood screws
(1¼", 2", 3½")

Galvanized common nails

Hammer

Eye protection

Sander

Spacers

Galvanized finish nails

Pneumatic narrow crown
stapler

Poultry netting
(chicken wire)

Galvanized U-nails

Aviation snips

Pliers

Galvanized butt hinges (6)

Galvanized T-hinges (2)

Galvanized latches (4)

Door Handle

How to Build a Chicken Ark

1 Make the eight rafters by laying out one rafter according to the diagram on page 118. Use this rafter as a template for marking and cutting the remaining rafters from 1 × 4 pine.

2 Cut an 8-ft. 1 × 8 to 86" to make the ridge pole. Cut at a bevel of 10 to 15° for a decorative tail cut at the roost end. Then, attach the rafters on one side of the ridge pole with 2" deck screws driven through the ridge pole and into the rafters. The rafters should be spaced according to the diagram (26" apart in the field area).

3 Attach the rafters on the opposite side of the ridge pole by driving 3½" deck screws through counterbored pilot holes in the rafter tops and into the ridge pole.

4 Attach the base plates to the bottom ends of the rafters with deck screws. The outside edges of the base plates should be flush with the outside edges of the rafters. Then, attach the spreader at each end of the framework. Make sure the rafter legs are spaced consistently.

5 Attach the roost beams between the legs of the outside rafters. The bottoms of the beams should be 14½ " up from the bottom of the ark. **TIP:** Before cutting the beams to size, hold the workpiece against the rafters to make sure it will fit. Attach the beams with 3½" deck screws predrilled and driven up toenail style through the bottom edges of the beams and into the rafters.

6 Attach the roost joist boards between the beam boards, flush against the inside edges of the rafters. Drive three 2" deck screws per joint.

7 Make the floor board for the roost. Cut the panel to size and then test the fit. Install the floor with pneumatic staples or screws driven into the beams and joists.

8 Cover the ark with galvanized metal poultry netting. Cut strips of netting to fit each side and then staple the netting with a pneumatic stapler and ⅞" narrow crown staples (otherwise, hand nail it with U-nails: A staple gun is inadequate for this job.) Trim the ends of the poultry netting (inset).

continued

How to Build a Chicken Ark (continued)

9 Cut the profiles onto the ends of the handles. Make a cardboard template of the profile and then trace the profile onto each end. Cut with a jigsaw and then sand the cuts and edges smooth.

10 Attach the carrying handles for the ark with 2" deck screws driven into pilot holes. The bottoms of the handles should be about 13" up from the bottom of the ark—make sure they are parallel to the base. Take care when drilling the pilot holes to keep them centered in the edges of the rafters. Make sure the handle end overhangs are equal and that the profiles are pointing upward.

11 Attach the roost side panels to the ark frame with pneumatic nails or staples or with 1¼" deck screws.

12 Install the end wall and the hinged roost door. The wall is affixed permanently with screws or staples. The door should be hinged from below. Install snap latches to the roost door fillers to secure the door in place when it is raised.

13 Make the frame for the ark door that fits against the open end of the ark. Rather than hinges, use latch hardware to hold the door in place. Begin by making the triangular door frame. Then, attach poultry netting to the exterior face of the door.

14 Complete the ark door by cutting and attaching the door brace and the door gusset and then securing the door against the end of the ark frame with latch hardware. Consider adding a utility handle to the gusset for ease of door handling.

15 Cut a 1 × 4 ridge board to span from the top of the ark door gusset to the beveled end of the ridge pole at the opposite end of the ark. Center the ridge board side to side and nail it to the ridge pole to cover the gaps.

16 Make the ramp and attach 1 × 2 battens to create purchase for the birds. Tip the coop up on end, then attach the ramp to one side of the roost floor with butt hinges. **TIP:** Drill a hole in the end of the ramp, tie a rope to it, and thread the rope out through the top of the ark so you can use it to raise and lower the ramp as needed.

123

Building a Beehive

Backyard beekeeping makes more sense today than ever before. Not only are honey bees necessary for pollinating plants and ensuring a better fruit set and bigger crops, they produce delicious honey and valuable beeswax. And recently, the world bee population has experienced a mysterious and concerning dropoff in numbers. Getting homeowners to cultivate a bee colony is a helpful component of the preservation strategy.

In many ways, tending bees is like growing food. There is an initial flurry of activity in spring, followed by ongoing maintenance in the summer and then harvest in the fall. There is prep work you'll need to complete before you begin and there is a learning curve—you'll need to spend more time with your bees in the beginning until you learn how it's done. Beekeeping is not necessarily an expensive hobby, but with higher-end operations, purchasing the hive, some blue ribbon bees, and all the necessary equipment can require a significant financial investment.

Keeping bees will help you have a better garden, more fruits and vegetables, and honey in the kitchen—even beeswax candles, skin creams, and other natural cosmetics. And, by building a top-bar beehive, you're creating a safe home and enabling one of our earth's most necessary and miraculous species to thrive.

Honey and beeswax are the two commodities a functioning backyard beehive will yield. If your primary interest is honey, build a traditional stacking-box style beehive in which the bees expend most of their energy filling the premade combs with sweet honey. If it's beeswax you seek, make a top-bar hive like the one shown on the following pages.

T I P   **5 Ways to Keep Your Bees Safe & Healthy**

1. Avoid using insecticides in your garden—Many are long-lasting and toxic to bees.

2. Buy seeds that are not treated with insecticides—Some coated seeds may cause the entire plant to become toxic to bees. Check seed packets carefully.

3. Mix your own potting soil and compost—Some composts and potting mixes sold at garden centers contain insecticide that is highly toxic to bees and other insects, and will eventually pollute all of your soil. Make your own compost, and mix with natural additives for potting plants.

4. Plant bee-friendly flowers—Buy wildflower seed mix and plant in uncultivated areas to create small sections of wild, natural habitat for your bees.

5. Provide a home for bees—Whether you're a blossoming beekeeper or not, it's easy to provide a home for bees! Provide a simple box as a place for feral bees to nest, or start your own hive.

○ Top-Bar Hive

Expert beekeeper Phil Chandler insists that beekeeping should be a very simple pursuit, largely because the bees do almost all of the work for you. Chandler, who maintains a Website called The Barefoot Beekeeper (See Resources, page 158), is an advocate for natural beekeeping and has designed a top-bar hive that you can build yourself using simple materials. This hive (see pages 127 to 129) is designed to enable the bees to build their own comb, instead of relying on a premade comb.

The top-bar hive is simple in its construction and, unlike the traditional stacked box Langstroth hive, does not require that you lift heavy boxes to check on your hive's progress, which disturbs the bees within. Rather, you can simply remove the hive roof and inspect the bars one by one without disturbing the rest of the hive. Storage is minimal for a top-bar hive, as there are no supers needed. And, it is not necessary with this hive design to isolate the queen.

This simple top-bar beehive design is a warm and safe home for bees that is easily adjustable to accommodate a growing hive. This design also greatly simplifies the inspection process and minimizes the amount of equipment needed to keep and maintain bees.

Building a Top-bar Beehive

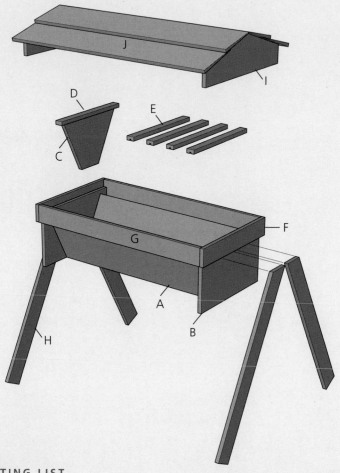

TOOLS & MATERIALS

Lumber (1 × 2, 1 × 3, 2 × 4, 1 × 12)

Carpenter's square

Pencil

Circular saw or table saw

Socket wrench

Exterior-grade construction adhesive

Caulk gun

Clamps

Drill

Tape measure

Hammer

Handsaw

1¼", 2", 2½" deck screws

Stainless-steel mesh

Rooting nails or narrow crown staples

Eye protection

1" holesaw

⅜ x 2" galv. lag bolts with washers and nuts

Molten beeswax

CUTTING LIST

Key	Part	No.	Dimension	Material
A	Side panel	2	¾ x 11¼ x 36"	Cedar
B	End panel	2	¾ x 11¼ x 19"	Cedar
C	Insert	2	¾ x 11¼ x 15"	Cedar
D	Insert cap	2	¾ x 1½ x 17"	Cedar
E	Top Bar	20	¾ x 1½ x 17"	Cedar
F	Frame end	2	¾ x 3½ x 21"	Cedar
G	Frame side	2	¾ x 3½ x 36"	Cedar
H	Leg	4	¾ x 1½ x 36"	Cedar
I	Cap end	2	¾ x 7¼ x 23"	Cedar
J	Roofing	6	⅝ x 5⅞ x 40"	Cedar bevel lap siding

How to Build a Top Bar Beehive

1 Lay out cutting lines for the insert panels on a piece of 1 × 12 cedar stock. The trapezoid-shaped panels (sometimes called followers) are meant to slide back and forth within the hive cavity, much like a file folder divider. This allows the beekeeper to subdivide the hive space as the honeycombs accumulate. The shape should be 15" wide along the top and 5" wide along the bottom (See diagram, page 127).

2 Cut the insert panels to size and shape and then attach a top cap to the top edge of each panel. The 1 × 2 caps, installed with the flat surface down, should overhang the panels by 1" at each end. Use exterior-rated wood glue and 2" deck screws driven through pilot holes to attach the tops. Also cut 20 top bars from the same 1 × 25. Use a router or table saw to cut a ¼ × ¼" groove in the bottom of each top bar (inset). The bees use these grooves to create purchase for their hanging honeycombs.

3 Secure the two insert panels upside down on a flat worksurface and use them to register the side panels so you can trace the panel locations onto the end panels. Center the end panels against the ends of the side panels, making sure the overhang is equal on each side. Outline the side panel locations, remove the end panels, and drill pilot holes in the outlined area.

4 Attach the end panels to the side panels with glue and 2½" deck screws driven through the pilot holes in the end panels.

5 Cut the parts for the frame that fits around the top of the hive box and fasten them with glue and 1¼" deck screws. The top of the frame should be slightly more than ¾" above the tops of the side panels to provide clearance for the top bars, which will rest on the side panel edges.

6 Attach the legs. First, cut 36"-long legs from 1 × 4 stock and place them over the box ends as shown in the diagram on page 127. Mark cutting lines where the leg tops intersect with the bottom of the frame. If your hive will be on grass or dirt, leave the bottom ends uncut to create a point that will help stabilize the hive. If your hive will be on a hard surface, cut the ends so they are parallel to the tops and will rest flush on the ground. Attach the legs with two or three ⅜ × 2" galvanized lag bolts fitted with washers and nuts.

7 Drill entrance holes and attach the box bottom. On one side panel, drill three 1"-dia. bee entrance holes 2" up from the bottom of the hive. One hole should be centered end to end and the others located 3" away from the center. On the other side, drill a 1"-dia. hole 2" up from the bottom of the hive and 5" from each end. Attach a steel or plastic mesh bottom with roofing nails or narrow crown staples.

8 Make and install the lid. You can design just about any type of covering you like. Here, a frame with a gable peak is made from cedar stock and then capped with beveled-lap siding (also cedar). The overlap area where the siding fits along the peak ridge should be sealed with clear exterior caulk. Add the inserts and top bars and then fit the lid frame around the box top frame.

Solar Electricity

When NASA scientists of the 1950s needed a revolutionary source of power for their spacecraft, they had to look and think beyond the earth. Their challenge was monumental, yet their solution poetically simple: They would find a way to tap into the most abundant, most accessible, and most reliable source of energy in the universe—the sun.

Producing your own electricity with photovoltaics, or PV, is certainly one of the most exciting and rewarding ways of going green. And in addition to electrical power, homeowners everywhere are using the sun to heat water for their showers, heating systems, and even swimming pools. The economic benefits can be significant, and when you consider that supplying the average home with conventional power creates over three tons of carbon emissions each year (over twice that of the average car), the environmental benefits of pollution-free solar energy are nothing to squint at.

This chapter introduces you to the most popular solar options for supplementing your existing systems or even declaring energy independence by taking your home "off the grid." As solar technology continues its journey from the space program to suburban rooftops and beyond, anyone serious about climbing aboard will find a vibrant new marketplace that's more than ready to help.

New solar products have made it easier to be green in urban locations. Here, slim solar panels are secured to a homeowner's balcony in the city.

Made with lightweight materials and highly durable materials, today's low-profile solar panels are ideal for discreet rooftop installation.

Solar cells: building blocks for a future of clean energy.

○ Solar for Electricity

Residential PV systems supply electricity directly to a home through solar panels mounted on the roof or elsewhere. These are essentially the same systems that pioneering homeowners installed back in the 1970s, except in those days panels were less efficient and much more expensive—to the tune of over $300 per watt in setup costs compared to around $9 per watt today (and people in many areas can cut that number in half with renewable energy rebates and tax credits).

Here's how PV power works: A solar panel is made up of small solar cells, each containing a thin slice of silicon, the same stuff used widely in the computer industry. Silicon is an abundant natural resource extracted from the earth's crust. It has semi-conductive properties, so that when light strikes the positive side of the slice, electrons try to move to the negative side. By connecting the two sides with a wire, you create an electrical circuit and a means for harnessing this electrical activity.

Solar cells are grouped together and connected by wires to create a module, or panel. Modules can be installed in a series to create a solar "array." The size of an array, as well as the quality of the semiconductor material, determines its power output.

The electricity produced by solar cells is DC, or direct current, which is what most batteries produce and what battery-powered devices run on. Most household appliances and light fixtures run on AC, or alternating current, electricity. Therefore, PV systems include an inverter that converts the DC power from the panels to AC power for use in the home. It's all the same to your appliances, and they run just as well on solar-generated power as on standard utility power.

Grid-Connected & Off-the-Grid Systems

Home PV systems can be designed to connect to the local utility network (the power grid) or to supply the home with all of its electricity without grid support. There are advantages and disadvantages to each configuration.

In a grid-connected setup, the utility system serves as a backup to supply power when household demand exceeds the solar system's capacity or during the hours when the sun is down. This obviates the need for batteries or a generator for backup and makes grid-connected systems simpler and less expensive than off-the-grid systems. One of the best advantages of grid connection is that when the solar system's output exceeds the house's demand, it delivers power back to the grid and you (may) get credit for every watt produced. This is called net-metering and is guaranteed by law in many states; however, not every state requires utility companies to offer it, and not all companies offer the same payback. Some simply let the meter roll backwards, essentially giving you full retail value for the power, while others buy back power at the utility's standard production price—much less than what they charge consumers.

The main drawbacks of being tied to the grid are that you may still have to pay service charges for the utility connection even if your net consumption is zero, and you're still vulnerable to power outages at times when you're drawing from the grid. But the convenience of grid backup combined with the lower cost and reduced maintenance of grid-tied systems makes them the most popular choice among homeowners in developed areas.

Off-the-grid, or standalone, systems serve as the sole supply of electricity for a home. They include a large enough panel array to meet the average daily demand of the household. During the day, excess power is stored in a bank of batteries for use when the sun is down or when extended cloud cover results in low output. Most standalone systems also have a gas-powered generator as a separate, emergency backup.

For anyone building a new home in an undeveloped area, installing a complete solar system to provide your own power can be less expensive than having the utility company run a line out to the house (beyond a quarter-mile or so, new lines can be very costly). There are some maintenance costs, namely in battery replacement, but it's possible to

Grid-connected systems (top) rely on the utility company for supplemental and backup energy. Off-the-grid systems (bottom) are self-sufficient and must use batteries for energy storage and a generator (usually gas-powered) for backup supply.

save a lot of money in the long run, and never having to pay a single electric bill is deeply satisfying to off-the-grid homeowners.

As mentioned, off-the-grid systems are a little more complicated than grid-tied setups. There are the batteries to care for, and power levels have to be monitored to prevent excessive battery run-down and to know when generator backup is required. To minimize power demands, off-the-grid homes tend to be highly energy-efficient. Using super-efficient appliances and taking smaller steps like connecting electronics to power strips that can be switched off to prevent small but cumulative energy losses from devices running in "standby" mode enables homeowners to get by with smaller, less expensive solar arrays. If you're interested in taking your home off the grid, talk with as many experts and off-the-grid homeowners as you can. Their experiences can teach you invaluable lessons for successful energy independence.

Solar Panel Products

PV modules come in a range of types for different applications and power needs. The workhorse of the group is the glass- or plastic-covered rigid panel that can be mounted to the roof of a house or other structure, on an exterior wall, or on the ground at various distances from the house. Panel arrays can also be mounted onto solar-powered tracking systems that follow the sun for increased productivity.

Mounting solar arrays on the ground offers greater flexibility in placement when rooftop installation is impractical or prohibited by local building codes or homeowners associations.

Rigid modules, sometimes called framed modules, are designed to withstand all types of weather, including hail, snow, and extreme winds, and manufacturers typically offer warranties of 20 to 25 years. Common module sizes range in width from about 2 ft. to 4 ft. and in length from 2 ft. to 6 ft. Smaller modules may weigh less than 10 pounds, while large panels may be 30 to 50 pounds each.

In addition to variations in size, shape, wattage rating, and other specifications, standard PV modules can be made with two different types of silicon cells. Single crystalline cells contain a higher grade of silicon and offer the best efficiency of sunlight-to-electricity conversion—typically around 10% to 14%. Multicrystalline, or polycrystalline, cells are made with a less exacting and thus cheaper manufacturing process. Solar conversion of these is slightly less than single crystalline, at around 10% to 12%, but warranties on panels may be comparable. All solar cells degrade slowly over time. Standard single crystalline and multicrystalline cells typically lose 0.25% to 0.5% of their conversion efficiency each year.

Amorphous Solar Cells

Another group of solar products are made with amorphous, or thin-film, technology in which noncrystalline silicon is deposited onto substrates, such as glass or stainless steel. Some substrates are flexible, allowing for a range of versatile products, including

Installing solar panels over an arbor, pergola, or other overhead structure can create a unique architectural element. Here, panels over an arbor provide shade for a patio space while generating electricity for the house.

135

self-adhesive strips that can be rolled out and adhered to metal roofing and thin solar modules that install just like traditional roof shingles. Amorphous modules typically offer lower efficiency—around 5% to 7%—and a somewhat faster degradation of 1% or more per year.

The Economics of Going Solar

While the environmental benefits of solar electricity are obvious and irrefutable, most people looking into adding a new solar system need to examine the personal financial implications of doing so. PV systems cost only a small fraction of what they did 30 years ago, but they're still quite expensive. For example, a three-kilowatt system capable of supplying most or all of the electricity for a typical green home can easily cost $30,000 (before rebates and credits) and take 20 to 25 years to pay for itself in reduced energy bills. An off-the-grid system will cost even more. Nevertheless, depending on the many factors at play, going solar can be a sound investment with a potentially high rate of return.

One way to consider solar as an investment is to think of it as paying for a couple of decades' worth of electricity bills in advance. Thanks to the long warranties offered by manufacturers and the reliability of today's systems, the costs of maintenance on a system are predictably low. This means that most of your total expense goes toward the initial setup of the system. If you divide the setup cost (after rebates and credits) by the number of kilowatt hours (kWh) the system will produce over its estimated lifetime, you'll come up with a per-kWh price that you can compare against your current utility rate. Keep in mind that your solar rate, as it were, is locked in, while utility rates are almost certain to rise over the lifetime of your system.

Now, about those rebates and credits: In many areas, homeowners going solar can receive sizable rebates through state, local, or utility-sponsored programs, in addition to federal tax credits, as applicable. All told, these financial incentives can add up to 50% or more of the total setup cost of a new PV system. To find out about what incentives are available through any of these sources, check out the Database of State Incentives for Renewables & Efficiency, online at www.dsireusa.org. Established solar businesses in any given area are also very well informed about incentives available to local residents.

Here are some of the factors that tend to affect the cost of a PV system, its effectiveness or efficiency, and the homeowner's return on investment:

- The house and geographic location—how much sun reaches the house; the roof's slope and roofing material
- Electric utility rates and net-metering rates
- Increased home value—PV systems and other energy-saving upgrades can increase a home's resale value (often without raising the property value used for tax assessment)
- Loan rate, if the system is financed

With so many factors to consider, getting to the bottom line can be complicated. Full-service solar companies will perform a cost/benefit analysis to help potential customers make a decision based on the financial picture. Of course, you should always check their numbers and scrutinize any variables used. You can also learn a lot by talking to other homeowners in your area who have had similar systems installed. Are they getting the return they expected? Have their systems been reliable and low-maintenance? Would they change anything given the chance to do it over?

This fiber-cement shingle roof features an integrated array of shingles laminated with thin-film PV modules.

137

Working with Solar Professionals

Companies that provide solar equipment and system design, installation, and maintenance services are rising in number every year. A few of these were around during the lean years of the 1980s and '90s, but many more have sprouted up in the last decade or so. In any case, this is now a highly competitive industry, so you can, and should, expect great service at competitive prices.

The reputation and reliability of your local solar provider are important considerations, but perhaps more important is the stability of the original equipment manufacturers (OEMs) who produce the main parts of your system and who carry those long warranties. Many of these are large, well-established companies with expertise in energy and/or electronics, so it's a good bet they'll be around in 20 or 25 years to honor their product warranties. Always discuss warranties carefully with your solar provider.

At present, the solar industry really isn't set up for do-it-yourself system design and installation. Professional installation may run you around 15% of the total system cost—quite a low rate for the home improvement industry—and that amount is subject to rebates and credits, which are based on installed system prices.

Before giving you a quote for the system package, a solar provider will want to know about your home, what type of roofing you have, and what the southern exposure is like. To ballpark the size of system you'll need, they'll probably look at your utility bills from the past year and ask how much power you want to get from solar: Will it cover all household demand or just a portion of it? You may have to pay a fee to cover the provider's legwork required for working up an accurate quote.

Services likely to be included in a provider's system package are:

- Complete system design and installation
- Guarantees on workmanship/installation
- Obtaining building/electrical permits
- Coordinating hookup with utility company
- Obtaining rebates and credits
- Help with OEM warranty claims
- Lifetime technical support

Another thing to be aware of when comparing various providers' quotes, and in talking to other customers, is the actual output of a panel or array as opposed to its STC (or "name plate") wattage rating. Industry sources say the actual useable power of a system is typically about 75% of the rated power. This means that if your home needs three kilowatts of power your system should be rated for four kilowatts.

Solar for Hot Water & Heating

The science behind solar water heating is quite simple: If you've ever turned on a garden hose that's been left out in the sun (only to get extremely hot water when you expected cold), you pretty much get how it works. In a basic solar hot water system, water or an antifreeze fluid is circulated through rooftop collector units, then down into the house (or swimming pool) where it feeds a system to supply domestic hot water or to supplement space heating equipment.

Solar hot water systems are used in many different climates and are inexpensive and reliable enough to yield relatively quick financial returns in addition to long-term environmental benefits. For most homes, the solar system is used in conjunction with conventional heating equipment, such as a hot water heater or boiler, providing preheated water to the system to reduce its net energy use. On average, solar heaters for domestic hot water are most cost-effective when they supply around 70% of a home's hot water. Solar systems supplementing heating equipment are most cost-effective when designed to offset 40% to 80% of the home's annual demand.

Types of Hot Water Systems

The basic setup of a solar hot water system includes one or more collectors, a storage tank, various control devices, and a network of piping. Indirect systems circulate the same water or fluid through a continuous pipe loop and transfer heat via a heat exchanger. Direct systems run fresh water through the collector's piping and into the home for direct use.

Systems are also defined by their means of circulation. Active heaters use a pump to move the water or fluid mechanically; passive heaters move water without pumps, usually through the natural process of thermosyphoning: As the water in the collector heats up, it flows into a storage tank while cold water refills the collector tubes.

Solar heaters for domestic hot water may include a separate storage tank that feeds preheated water into a standard tank-style hot water heater or a tankless on-demand heater. The water heater can then boost the temperature of the water as needed. In other systems, solar-heated water is fed directly into a hot water tank, which typically contains its own conventional heat source.

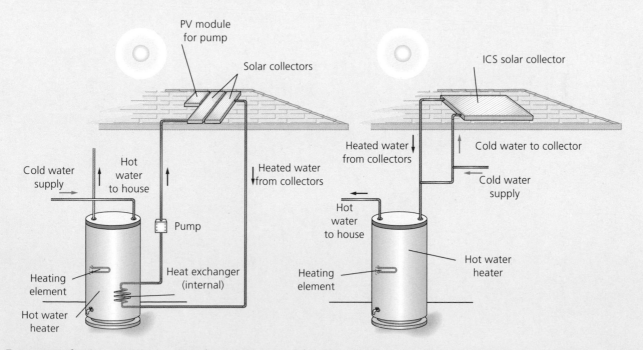

Two systems for domestic hot water: An indirect, active system (left) heats water via a heat exchanger inside a hot water tank and uses a pump to circulate fluid to and from the solar collectors. A direct, passive system (right) heats the same water that gets used in the house and relies on natural processes for circulation.

Solar Security Light Circuit

A self-contained electrical circuit with dedicated loads, usually 12-volt light fixtures, is one of the most useful solar amenities you can install. A standalone system is not tied into your power grid, which greatly reduces the danger of installing the components yourself. Plus, the fact that your light fixtures are independent of the main power source means that even during a power outage you will have functioning emergency and security lights.

Installing a single solar-powered circuit is relatively simple, but don't take the dangers for granted. Your work will require permits and inspections in most jurisdictions, and you can't expect to pass if the work is not done to the exact specifications required.

Solar panels that convert the sun's energy into electricity are called photovoltaic (PV) panels, and they produce direct current (DC) power. PV solar panel systems can be small and designed to accomplish a specific task, or they can be large enough to provide power or supplementary power to an entire family's home. Before you make the leap into a large system, it's a good idea to familiarize yourself with the mechanics of solar power. The small system demonstrated in this project is relatively simple and is a great first step into the world of solar. The fact that the collector, battery, and lights are a standalone system makes this a very easy project to accomplish. By contrast, **installing panels that provide direct supplementary power through your main electrical service panel is a difficult wiring job that should be done by professional electricians only.**

This 60-watt solar panel is mounted on a garage roof and powers a self-contained home security lighting system. Not only does this save energy costs, it keeps the security lights working even during power outages.

141

DC Light Circuit Schematic

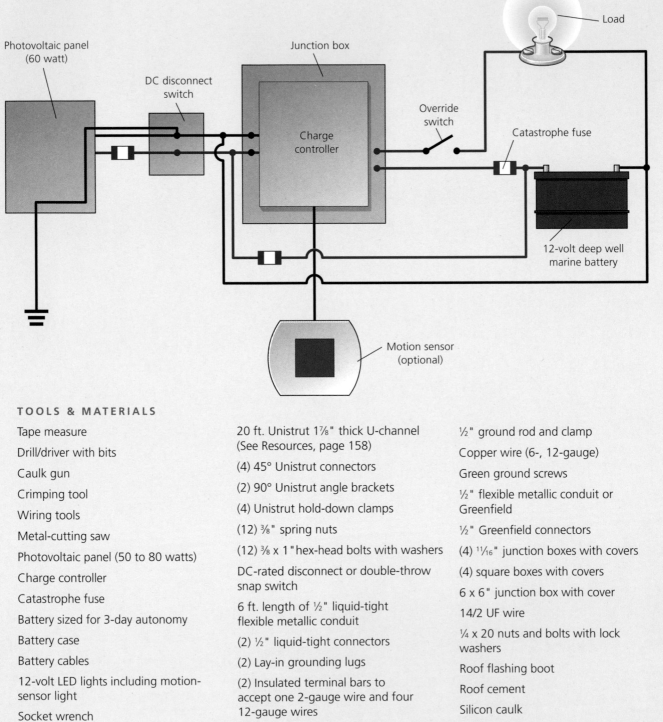

Photovoltaic panel (60 watt)

DC disconnect switch

Junction box

Load

Override switch

Catastrophe fuse

Charge controller

12-volt deep well marine battery

Motion sensor (optional)

TOOLS & MATERIALS

Tape measure

Drill/driver with bits

Caulk gun

Crimping tool

Wiring tools

Metal-cutting saw

Photovoltaic panel (50 to 80 watts)

Charge controller

Catastrophe fuse

Battery sized for 3-day autonomy

Battery case

Battery cables

12-volt LED lights including motion-sensor light

Socket wrench

20 ft. Unistrut 1⅞" thick U-channel (See Resources, page 158)

(4) 45° Unistrut connectors

(2) 90° Unistrut angle brackets

(4) Unistrut hold-down clamps

(12) ⅜" spring nuts

(12) ⅜ x 1" hex-head bolts with washers

DC-rated disconnect or double-throw snap switch

6 ft. length of ½" liquid-tight flexible metallic conduit

(2) ½" liquid-tight connectors

(2) Lay-in grounding lugs

(2) Insulated terminal bars to accept one 2-gauge wire and four 12-gauge wires

(2) Cord cap connectors for ½" cable

½" ground rod and clamp

Copper wire (6-, 12-gauge)

Green ground screws

½" flexible metallic conduit or Greenfield

½" Greenfield connectors

(4) ¹¹⁄₁₆" junction boxes with covers

(4) square boxes with covers

6 x 6" junction box with cover

14/2 UF wire

¼ x 20 nuts and bolts with lock washers

Roof flashing boot

Roof cement

Silicon caulk

○ Installing an Off-the-Grid Solar Lighting System

Before you begin installing a standalone solar-powered circuit, you'll need to make some basic determinations. The panel location is chief among these questions. Position the solar panel where it will receive the greatest amount of sunlight for the longest period of time each day—typically the south-facing side of a roof or wall. For a circuit with a battery reserve that powers two to four 12-volt lights, a collection panel rated between 40 and 80 watts of output should suffice. These panels can range from $200 to $600 in price, depending on the output and the overall quality.

Mounting the Panel

The photovoltaic panel must be securely mounted on a permanent stand and then connected via wires to the power distribution hardware inside the structure. Although some low-wattage panels come with a mounting stand, on larger PV panels you'll need to construct the mounting structure yourself using metal U-channels or other materials. The stand seen in this project is constructed with channels and fittings to secure the panel in a south-facing position on a garage roof. The structure is made with Unistrut brand metal channel and hardware (see Resources, page 158).

The mounting stand for the PV panel is constructed from metal U-channel and pre-bent fasteners. Electrical connections to the power distribution system are made inside the garage.

The stand components are held together with bolts and spring-loaded fasteners. The 45° and 90° connectors are manufactured specifically for use with this Unistrut system.

Connections for the feed wires that carry current from the collector are made inside an electrical box mounted on the back of the collector panel.

First, install two tracks of U-channel on the roof, parallel to the long edges of the panel. Attach the channels to the roof deck use the mounting hardware designed for your mounting system. Mount two 30° beam clamps onto the U-channel tracks to hold the panel at the best angle for maximum sunlight exposure.

Determine the location of the wire leads that penetrate the roof and will connect to the charge controller and battery. Mark the position for the leads onto the roof and use a ⅞" drill bit to bore an opening in the roof at this mark. Install a roof flange with a rubber boot over the opening and insert a section of ¾"-dia. PVC conduit into the boot. Seal all casing connections with silicon caulk.

Attach the panel to the stand beam clamps and thread the lead wires through the PVC conduit leading into the structure. Tighten all bolts securely. Check that the panel fits tightly into the clamps and does not move even slightly when agitated.

Make Interior Wiring Connections

Mount a junction box inside the building directly underneath the PVC conduit and wiring entry point, attaching it to a rafter or truss. Secure the box to the PVC conduit and seal with silicon caulk. Feed the lead wires from the PV panel into the junction box.

On a wall at roughly switch height, install a DC disconnect switch in a junction box. The disconnect switch allows you to shut off the flow of electrical current from the solar panel. Attach a junction box to enclose the DC disconnect to a wall stud near the battery

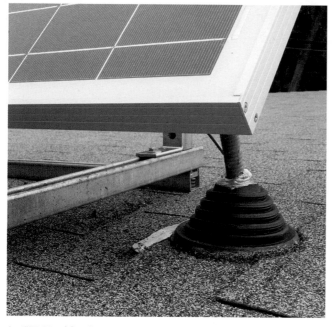

An **EPDM rubber boot** seals off the opening where the PVC conduit carrying the feed wires penetrates the roof.

The feed wires from the collector are fed into a junction box inside the structure where connections to the power distribution equipment are made.

and charge controller location. Run flexible metal conduit along the rafters or trusses and wall studs from the ceiling junction box to the DC disconnect box.

Attach a junction box beneath the DC disconnect box to enclose the charge controller. Connect the controller to the DC disconnect box with flexible metal conduit. Install the charge controller inside the box. About 2" away from the charge controller, mount a touch-safe fuse holder with a 10-amp "catastrophe" fuse as well.

Determine the placement of the battery and then decide where you will position the charge controller and DC disconnect nearby. The battery should be placed at least 18"off the floor in a well-ventilated area, where it won't be agitated by everyday activity.

Build the battery shelving. Securely attach the plastic battery casing to a plywood shelf with wood screws.

Set up grounding protection by pounding an 8-ft. long ground rod into the earth outside the building, about 1 foot from the wall on the opposite side of the charge controller. Leave about 2" of the rod sticking out of the ground. Attach a ground rod clamp to the top of the rod. Run a 6-gauge THWN wire from the ground rod to the bottom of the DC disconnect box. Cut the wire, leaving about 8" of length inside the DC disconnect box.

Run wiring from the disconnect switch to the ceiling junction box. Thread 6-gauge wire through the PVC conduit and attach it directly to a metal component of the PV panel. This wire will run down to the grounding rod for lightning protection.

Attach the two 14-gauge wires to the two terminals labeled "line" on the top of the DC disconnect switch. Route two more 14-gauge wires from the bottom of the DC

Catastrophe fuse

A 10-amp "catastrophe fuse" is inserted in the incoming current line to protect the fixtures from damaging power surges, most often the result of a lightning strike.

disconnect terminals into the junction box and connect to the "Solar Panel In" terminals on the charge controller. The black wire should connect to the negative terminal and the red to the positive. Screw a ground pigtail into the DC disconnect box and splice together both 6-gauge wires and the ground tail into a red wire connector.

Connect the charge controller to the battery. Run a 14-gauge wire from the charge controller output that goes to the battery to the line side of the touch-safe fuse. From the load side of the touch-safe fuse holder, run 14-gauge wire through the heavy-duty cable leading to the positive battery terminal location. Crimp the end to the eyelets of the battery casing. Crimp the negative battery terminal wire to the battery casing and route the wire through the second cable into another hole in the bottom of the charge controller junction box and connect to the charge controller at the designated location.

Install the lighting fixtures and hook them up to the power source with UF cable.

Make sure the disconnect switch is in the off position. Attach the crimped ends of the lead wires to the battery terminals and put the cover on the battery. At this point, label all wires and seek approval from your local building inspector. Connect the panel to the circuit. To stop the power flowing from the panel, cover it temporarily but securely with an opaque bag or blanket. Attach the black wire from the PV module to the negative lead and the red wire from the panel to the positive lead with yellow wire nuts. Fold the wires into the box and secure the cover onto the box. Remove the bag from the panel and turn the DC disconnect switch on to complete the circuit.

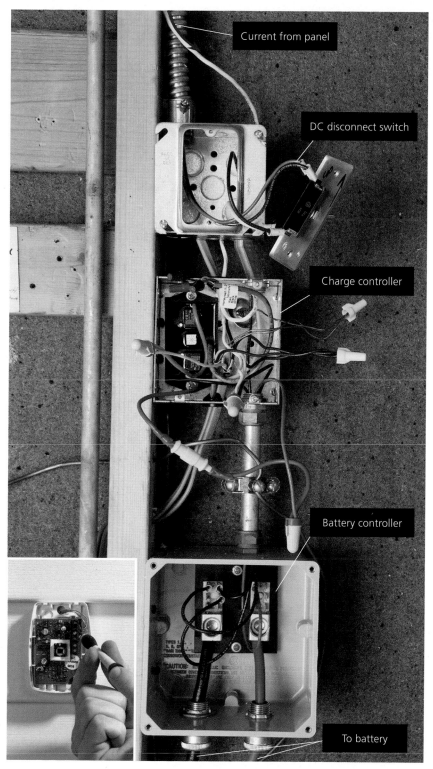

Current from panel

DC disconnect switch

Charge controller

Battery controller

To battery

The storage battery for the 12-volt system should be rated for three days of autonomous usage. Mount the battery in a sturdy plastic case that's at least 18 in. above ground.

The electrical components of the power processing system are wired in series through electrical boxes mounted inside the structure. The principal components include the disconnect switch (top box), a charge controller (middle box), and a battery controller (bottom box). An optional motion sensor (inset) triggers the lights.

Solar Heat

Most homes, and especially older ones, are beset by one stubborn room that just never quite warms up—whether it's a remote second floor bedroom, a kitchen or dining room with large, north-facing windows, or a main floor office in the corner closed off from the home's central heating system. Operating an electric space heater can help you warm up in the short-term, but is not an energy-efficient or long-term solution to this problem. One very efficient long-term solution, however, is to build and install hot-air solar panels. Even if you don't have a cold spot, a supplementary solar heat system can save plenty of energy dollars.

Using solar energy to heat a cold space in your home is a great way to harvest the sun's energy and supplement your home's heat in these problem areas. Solar hot air panels are fundamentally different than photovoltaic panels—this style is designed to use the sun's energy to heat the air inside each box rather than to create electricity. Mounted on a south-facing wall or on the roof, solar hot air panels collect air from inside your home and blow or draw it through the thermal solar panels, which are essentially a series of metal ducts in a black box under tempered glass. As the air moves through the ductwork, the sun's rays cause it to heat to high temperatures. Then, at the end of the duct, another vent moves the air back into your home's heating ductwork or an interior vent, sending the now-heated air right into the home.

When combined, these three DIY "hotboxes" introduce enough hot air into this home to carry 30 to 40% of the home heating load.

149

You can build solar hot air panels yourself. This style seen here is simple: essentially, a box, a series of ducts, and a piece of glass. The panels are permanently installed and ducted in to your home, complete with automated thermostatic controls. In this project, we'll walk you through one version of a solar hot air panel designed and installed by Applied Energy Innovations of Minneapolis, Minnesota (see Resources p. 158), with the help of homeowner Scott Travis.

Anatomy of a Hot Air Solar Panel

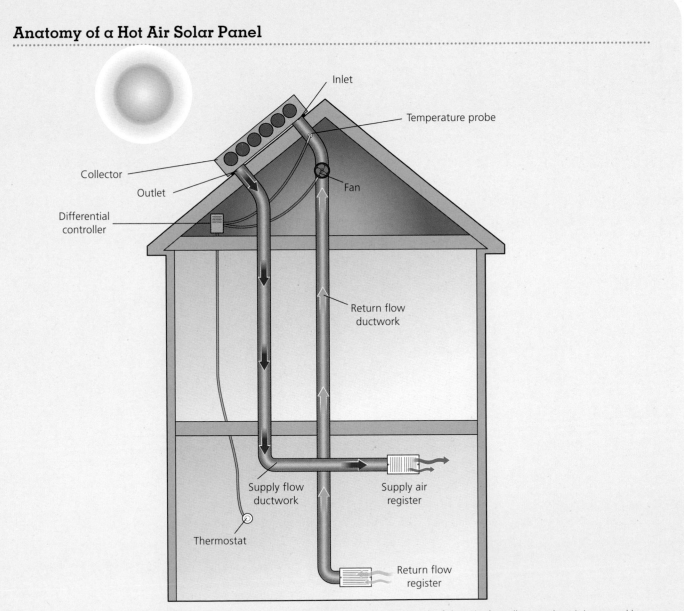

The solar hot box is a very simple system. Cold air from the house is drawn up into a network of ducts in the collector, where it is warmed by the sun then circulated inside to heat the house.

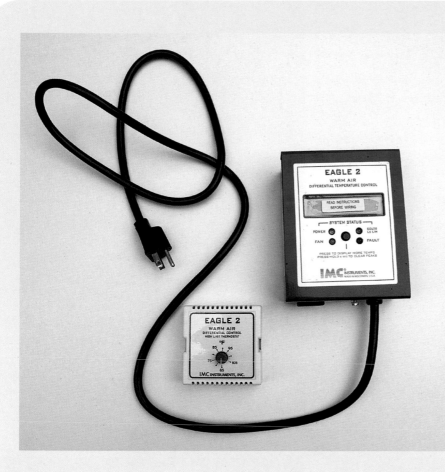

The temperature control equipment opens and closes the damper and causes the blower fan to turn on and off as needed.

TOOLS & MATERIALS

Jigsaw or circular saw with metal-cutting blade

Drywall saw

Straightedge

Aviation snips

Tape measure

Eye and ear protection

Carpenter's square

Drill/driver with bits

⅛" pop rivets

Pop rivet gun

High-temperature silicon caulk

Caulk gun

Aluminum foil tape

1"-thick R7 rigid insulation

2 x 6 steel studs

Utility knife

Tempered glass

4" hole saw

Sheet-metal start collars

8" plenum box (2)

4" male and female duct connectors

1"-wide closed-cell foam gasket

4" aluminum HVAC duct

High-temperature black paint (matte)

Trim paint roller

Sheet-metal screws with rubber gaskets

Chalkline

Cardboard

Scissors

Reciprocating saw

Roof jack

Roofing cement

Flashing

Rubber gasket rooting nails

Shingles (if needed)

Unistrut

Unistrut connectors

Duct collars (2)

⅜" threaded rod

Spring-fed 8" backdraft dampers

8" blower fan

Temperature controls

How to Build a Solar Hot Air Panel

1 Cut and bend the box frame pieces from 2 × 6 steel studs. Each steel stud piece will wrap two sides of the panel with a 90° corner bend. Mark the bend location on both steel studs. Cut a relief cut into the 6" side of the stud with aviation snips at this mark. Bend the stud to an L-shape and use a square to ensure that the corner forms a true 90° angle.

2 Drill ⅛"-dia. holes in the overlapping top and bottom flanges. Clamp the corners together before drilling and use a square to make sure the corner forms a 90° angle.

3 Fasten the corners of the metal box with two ⅛"-dia. sheet-metal pop rivets in the top and bottom. Leave one corner open to create access for the insulation panel insert.

4 Cut the foil-faced rigid foam insulation to match the interior dimensions of the box, using a drywall saw or a utility knife.

5 Apply high-temperature silicon to the bottom flanges of the box (inset). Fit the 1" foil-face rigid foam insulation into the back of the frame, then close up the box and secure the open corner. Cut 5"-wide strips of foam insulation to the length and width of the panel. Place a thick bead of silicon around the outside perimeter of the unit. Insert the strips into the silicon and tightly against the sides of the panel to hold the backing firmly in place. The foil should be facing into the box.

6 Seal the insulation edges. Place a bead of silicon around the inside corner where the insulation strips and backing panel meet, and then seal with foil tape. Flip the panel over. Place a bead of silicon on the intersection of the 2×6 stud flange and the back of the insulation and seal with foil tape. Conceal any exposed insulation edges with foil tape.

7 Create inlet and outlet holes in the walls with a hole saw or circle cutter. The number and location of the ductwork holes depends on where each panel fits into the overall array (presuming you are making and installing multiple panels). The first and last panels in the series each will have one end wall that is uncut, while intermediate panels will have duct holes on each end wall (inset).

8 Install a compartment separator in the first and last panels with a piece of foil insulation set on edge. Cut ductwork access holes in the separator. Then, cut out holes for the ductwork that will pass through the separator. Also cut a plenum opening in the separated compartment in the first and last unit.

continued

How to Build a Solar Hot Air Panel (continued)

9 Paint the entire box interior black using high-temperature paint and allow it to dry completely. A trim roller works well for this task.

10 Insert the ductwork. Beginning at the plenum over the inlet duct, guide 4" aluminum HVAC ductwork in a serpentine shape throughout the entire multi-panel installation, ending at the outlet duct. Join ends of adjoining duct sections with flexible duct connectors fashioned into a U shape and secured with metal screws and foil tape (inset). Paint each section of ductwork with black high-temperature paint once it is in place.

11 Paint the last section of ductwork and touch up around the interior of the box so all exposed surfaces are black.

12 Affix the glass top. First, double check that all openings in the panel are adequately sealed and insulated. Then, line the tops of the steel stud frame with foam closed-cell gasket tape. Carefully position the glass on top of the gasket tape, lined up ½" from the outside of the frame on all sides. Then, position foam closed-cell gasket tape around the perimeter of the top of the glass panel.

13 Attach the casing. Work with a local metal shop to bend metal flashing that will wrap your panel box. Attach around the perimeter of the panel with sheet-metal screws with rubber washer heads. **TIP:** Be careful when working around the plenum ductwork. If you set the unit down on its backside, you will force the plenum up and break the seal around the opening.

14 Mark off the panel layout locations on the roof. Transfer the locations of the 8"-dia. inlet and outlet holes to the roof as well. The location of these holes should not interfere with the structural framing members of your roof (either rafters or trusses). Adjust the panel layout slightly to accommodate the best locations of the inlet and outlet, according to your roof's setup. Cut out the inlet and outlet holes with a reciprocating saw.

15 Use a roof jack or Cone-jack to form an 8"-dia. opening. Apply a heavy double bead of roofing cement along the top and sides of the roof jack. Nail the perimeter of the flange using rubber gasket nails. Cut and install shingles with roofing cement to fit over the flashing so they lie flat against the flange.

16 Attach Unistrut mounting U-channel bars to the roof for each panel. Use the chalklines on the roof to determine the position of the Unistrut, and attach to the roof trusses with Unistrut connectors.

continued

How to Build a Solar Hot Air Panel (continued)

18 Connect the panels to the Unistrut with ⅜" threaded rod attached at the top and bottom of the panel on the outside. Cut threaded rod to size, then attach to the Unistrut with Unistrut nuts. Attach the top clip to the top of the rod and the front face of the panel. Tighten the assembly to compress the panel down to the Unistrut for a tight hold. Seal the panel connections with 1" foam gasket tape around each end of the panels where they connect. Place a bead of silicon caulk on top of the gasket tape and then attach 3"-wide flashing over the two panels at the joint. Attach flashing to the panel with galvanized sheet metal screws with rubber gasket heads.

17 Hoist the panels into position. Carefully follow safety regulations and use scaffolding, ladders, ropes, and lots of helpers to hoist the panels onto the roof. Wear fall-arresting gear and take care not to allow the plenum ductwork to be damaged. Connect the inlet and outlet ducts on the panel(s) to the openings on the roof (inset). Position the panels so the inlet and outlet openings match perfectly, and attach with a duct collar and silicon caulk.

19 Hook up the interior ductwork, including dampers and a blower fan. The manner in which this is done will vary tremendously depending on your house structure and how you plan to integrate the supplementary heat. You will definitely want to work with a professional HVAC contractor (preferably one with experience with solar) for this part of the job.

Conversions

Metric Equivalent

Inches (in.)	1/64	1/32	1/25	1/16	1/8	1/4	3/8	2/5	1/2	5/8	3/4	7/8	1	2	3	4	5	6	7	8	9	10	11	12	36	39.4
Feet (ft.)																								1	3	3 1/12
Yards (yd.)																									1	1 1/12
Millimeters (mm)	0.40	0.79	1	1.59	3.18	6.35	9.53	10	12.7	15.9	19.1	22.2	25.4	50.8	76.2	101.6	127	152	178	203	229	254	279	305	914	1,000
Centimeters (cm)							0.95	1	1.27	1.59	1.91	2.22	2.54	5.08	7.62	10.16	12.7	15.2	17.8	20.3	22.9	25.4	27.9	30.5	91.4	100
Meters (m)																								.30	.91	1.00

Converting Measurements

To Convert:	To:	Multiply by:
Inches	Millimeters	25.4
Inches	Centimeters	2.54
Feet	Meters	0.305
Yards	Meters	0.914
Miles	Kilometers	1.609
Square inches	Square centimeters	6.45
Square feet	Square meters	0.093
Square yards	Square meters	0.836
Cubic inches	Cubic centimeters	16.4
Cubic feet	Cubic meters	0.0283
Cubic yards	Cubic meters	0.765
Pints (U.S.)	Liters	0.473 (Imp. 0.568)
Quarts (U.S.)	Liters	0.946 (Imp. 1.136)
Gallons (U.S.)	Liters	3.785 (Imp. 4.546)
Ounces	Grams	28.4
Pounds	Kilograms	0.454
Tons	Metric tons	0.907

To Convert:	To:	Multiply by:
Millimeters	Inches	0.039
Centimeters	Inches	0.394
Meters	Feet	3.28
Meters	Yards	1.09
Kilometers	Miles	0.621
Square centimeters	Square inches	0.155
Square meters	Square feet	10.8
Square meters	Square yards	1.2
Cubic centimeters	Cubic inches	0.061
Cubic meters	Cubic feet	35.3
Cubic meters	Cubic yards	1.31
Liters	Pints (U.S.)	2.114 (Imp. 1.76)
Liters	Quarts (U.S.)	1.057 (Imp. 0.88)
Liters	Gallons (U.S.)	0.264 (Imp. 0.22)
Grams	Ounces	0.035
Kilograms	Pounds	2.2
Metric tons	Tons	1.1

Converting Temperatures

Convert degrees Fahrenheit (F) to degrees Celsius (C) by following this simple formula: Subtract 32 from the Fahrenheit temperature reading. Then mulitply that number by $\frac{5}{9}$. For example, 77°F - 32 = 45. 45 $\times$ $\frac{5}{9}$ = 25°C.

To convert degrees Celsius to degrees Fahrenheit, multiply the Celsius temperature reading by $\frac{9}{5}$, then add 32. For example, 25°C $\times$ $\frac{9}{5}$ = 45. 45 + 32 = 77°F.

Fahrenheit   **Celsius**

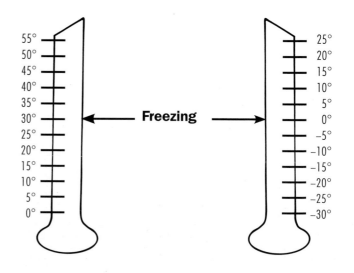

Resources

AEE Solar
800-777-6609
www.aeesolar.com

Applied Energy Innovations
612-532-0384
www.appliedenergyinnovations.org
Pages 141 and 149

Atkinson Electronics
800-261-3602
atkinsonelectronics.com

The Barefoot Beekeeper
www.biobees.com
Page 126

Earthtronics and Honeywell
866-6-EARTH-0
www.earthtronics.com/honeywell.aspx

Envirosink
888-663-4950
www.envirosink.com
Page 19

Flotender
800-906-0604
www.flotender.com

Unistrat Metal Framing
800-521-7730
www.unistrat.us
Page 143

Wind Powering America
www.windpoweringamerica.gov

Credits

Molly Joy Matheson Gruen
Peace Photography
p. 96 (pigs and goats)

Shutterstock, pp. 35, 41 both, 54, 55, 78,
79, 84, 85, 90, 92, 102, 117 right, 124

iStockphoto, p. 82

Index

A

Alternative energy, 6, 8

B

Beekeeping, 124–126
  building a top-bar
    beehive, 127–129
Boosting your garden's yield,
  building a cold frame, 48–53
  building a greenhouse, 58–67
    where to site, 60–61
  building a hoophouse, 68–77
    where to site, 70

C

Canning food, 79, 81–83
  process, 83
  safety, 82, 83
Collecting gray water, 7, 18–21
  installing a gray water recovery
    sink, 20–21
Collecting rainwater, 9, 12–17
  rain barrels, 14
  making a rain barrel, 15–17
Container gardening, 38–47
  building planter boxes, 43–45
  building a strawberry
    barrel, 9, 46–47
Composting, 6
  building a compost
    bin, 6, 26–30
  managed composting, 23

variables, 24–25
  what to compost, what not to
    compost, 31

D

Drying produce, 9, 79, 81, 84–91
  electric food dryer, 90
  solar food dryer, 87
    building a, 88–89
  on trays, 86
  pasteurization and storage, 91
  using your oven, 90

F

Food preservation, 78–91
  choosing the best method, 80
Freezing your produce, 81

L

Living "Green," 5, 6

P

Producing your own food, 8, 9
  starting and transplanting
    seedlings, 55–57

R

Raised garden beds, 32–37
  bed positions, 33
  companion planting, 34–35
  how to build, 36–37

soil, 35

    watering, 35

Raising animals, 102–113

    alpacas, 107

    fencing and shelter, 104–105,
108–113

        building a post and board
fence, 110–111

        building a Virginia rail
fence, 112–113

    goats, 106

    pigs, 106

    sheep, 107

Raising chickens, 103

    building a chicken arc, 103,
115–123

    building a chicken coop, 8

Root cellars, 81, 93–101

    how to store produce in
a cellar, 94

    setting up in a basement, 96–99

    setting up a root cellar
shelf, 100–101

S

Saving in utility costs, 8, 136

Self-sufficient lifestyle, 6–8

Solar electricity, 6–7, 131–139

    building a solar panel, 6

    grid-connected and off-the-grid
systems,133–134

Solar heat, 148–156

    for hot water and heating, 139

Solar panels, 149–150

    anatomy of a, 150

    building a solar hot air panel,
151–135

    products, 134–135

Solar security light circuit,
140–147

    installing an off-the-grid solar
lighting system, 143–144